MARK WILSON'S GREATEST
CARD
TRICKS

An imprint of Running Press
Philadelphia • London

ACKNOWLEDGMENTS

The contents of this book do not represent the efforts of only two, three, or a dozen individuals; rather, they represent all those magicians of the past and the present who have labored so diligently to create, perfect, and present the Art of Magic.

Just as a stalagmite, buried unseen in a dark cave, builds from tiny drops into a towering structure, so has our Art increased through the centuries, shrouded in a like darkness of secrecy which remains a prerequisite to its growth.

With this book, you will join the ranks of those who have learned these inner secrets—and you must acknowledge and respect those whose contributions we enjoy. *Acknowledge* by being aware of the countless hours of study, work, and practice that have been expended by the magicians of the past to create our Art. *Respect* the magicians of today by never revealing any of these hard-earned secrets.

This, then, is the grateful acknowledgment of this book: *to the Magicians of all times and places,* for their countless contributions to the Art of Magic.

9 8 7 6 5 4 3 2
Digit on the right indicates the number of this printing.

Library of Congress Cataloging-in-Publication Number 93-70588

ISBN 1-56138-335-X

Compiled by Caroline Schweiter
Edited by Liz Kaufman
Jacket design by Toby Schmidt
Jacket photography by Weaver Lilley
Interior design by Ruthie Thompson

Published by Courage Books, an imprint of
Running Press Book Publishers
125 South Twenty-second Street
Philadelphia, Pennsylvania 19103

Printed in Hong Kong.
MA-022C

TABLE OF CONTENTS

MARK WILSON

Because of his numerous television appearances around the world, it is estimated that Mark Wilson has performed magic for more people than any magician in the 3,500-year history of the art.

♦ Starred in first weekly network magic series, *"Magic Land of Allakazam,"* which aired two years on CBS, three years on ABC networks; six *"Magic Circus"* specials; *"Magic of Mark Wilson"* syndicated series; four HBO Magic Specials; *"Magic of China," "Children of China," "Mr. Magic"* syndicated specials; and many more.

♦ International programming includes television specials for the NHK, NTV and ASAHI *Japanese Networks* and for *Korea, Canada, Hong Kong, Australia, Great Britain,* and *People's Republic of China.* Wilson's U.S. productions have aired throughout *South America, Europe, Southeast Asia, Pacific Rim Countries,* and elsewhere.

♦ Creative consultant and supplier of magic to countless television series, such as *Columbo, Simon and Simon, Love Boat, Circus of the Stars, Perfect Strangers, Dear John, The Odd Couple,* and many more.

♦ Instructs Hollywood's top stars in the performance of magic. Past and present celebrity students include *Cary Grant, Tony Curtis, Peter Falk, Bill Bixby, Jackie Gleason, Cher, Johnny Carson, Burt Reynolds,* and many others.

♦ First foreign magician to perform in mainland China since the founding of the *People's Republic of China,* in history-making 1980 performing tour.

♦ Prepares entertainment packages for many of the world's finest *theme parks, world's fairs, expositions, and major corporations* worldwide.

♦ World's most honored magician with <u>two</u> prestigious *"Magician Of The Year"* and *"Master's Fellowship"* from Academy of Magical Arts, *"Superstar of Magic," "Magician of the Decade," "Lifetime Achievement,"* and many other national and international awards.

INTRODUCTION

Card tricks have always held a fascination for audiences. During the past century, literally thousands of tricks, sleights, and routines have been invented for playing cards. Certainly there has been more innovation, invention, and diversity in card tricks than any other category of magic. Some card tricks are easy to do; others require intricate sleight-of-hand. But, no matter what methods are used, just about everyone likes a good card trick.

Perhaps one reason card magic is so popular is that audiences can identify with the props—in other words, everyone knows what a deck of cards is, and most people have handled cards, whether they were gambling, playing bridge, or sticking the ace of spades between the spokes of a bicycle.

I speak from experience when I tell you that sometimes a good card trick will have more impact on an audience than "sawing a lady in half"! As a practical matter, card tricks are wonderful. You can easily carry a deck of cards with you wherever you go and perform in almost any situation—neither of which can be said for dividing a young lady in two.

In this book, I have compiled a wide assortment of tricks. Some are simple and use an unprepared deck; others require a little practice. Still others use special "trick cards," which you can make yourself or pick up at a local magic shop.

It is important that you don't ignore the simple, self-working card tricks. Just because a trick is easy to do does not mean it is less effective than a more complicated trick. And don't be in a hurry to learn all the tricks at once. Begin by learning a few simple tricks, then practice them until you feel comfortable. Try them out on your family and friends, refine them, hone them to perfection, and then move on. Remember, you want to have fun and fool your friends. Never take a chance of ruining a good trick just because you haven't practiced it well enough.

Once you have mastered a few tricks, think about different ways they can be presented. You'll notice that several card tricks may utilize one or more of the same secrets, but the effect of each trick to an audience is totally different. Perhaps that's one of the greatest advantages to card magic: you can suit each trick to fit your personality, your audience, and the performing conditions. And don't forget to be creative.

Just use your imagination—you'll be amazed what you can come up with!

Mark Wilson

CARD MAGIC

Tricks with cards form their own branch of magic. In fact, due to the wide range of opportunities, there are some magicians who specialize entirely in card tricks.

From the moment you start doing card tricks, you naturally acquire a manipulative ability. The acts of cutting, shuffling, and dealing a pack of cards demand skill. When you spread the pack and invite someone to "take a card," or when you run rapidly through the face-up pack looking for the cards needed for some special trick, you acquire further facility. Next, you may find fancy cuts and flourishes to your liking; and if you do, you will be on the road to becoming a card expert almost before you realize it.

There are many tricks involving the discovery of cards selected by members of the audience. These depend upon a variety of methods that enable you to keep a jump ahead of keen-eyed and keen-witted spectators. Basically, there are three ways of discovering a chosen card. One is to "force" it on the spectator, so that you know the card beforehand and therefore can predict it, name it, or produce a duplicate from some unexpected place. Another is to "locate" the card by its position in the pack, so you can find it by simply looking through the pack or studying the cards as you deal them. The third way is to "control" the chosen card by shuffles, cuts, and other manipulations that enable you to reveal it at any time.

All three ways are covered in this book. Each has its own variations, depending on different degrees of skill. By switching from one method to another, you can leave your audiences utterly nonplussed. You will be further aided by a special device called a "short" card, which you can find or control by the sense of touch alone.

By adding some of the more elaborate effects described in this book, you can soon round out a program of card magic that will stand as a complete act in itself.

CHAPTER 1

CARD-HANDLING TECHNIQUES

Throughout all card magic, you will find that there are certain basic card-handling techniques which are essential to your ability to perform tricks. These include shuffling and dealing. These techniques will not necessarily appear in each card trick, but there are very few tricks that do not require at least a shuffle.

You probably already know one, but you will find that there are several kinds of shuffles. Most of them serve some special purpose, such as controlling the position of a card. Together, they give you the opportunity to introduce variety into your card handling.

Similarly, there are different techniques for dealing. The success of a trick frequently depends on your skillful accomplishment of this manipulation. Therefore, you are urged to practice all of the following manipulations until you can do each one smoothly, confidently, and without hesitation.

Remember, the mere appearance of skill and confidence in your handling of cards will add much to your audience's respect for your ability as a magician.

RIFFLE SHUFFLE

 The riffle shuffle is probably the most widely used method of shuffling cards. For that reason alone, you should be familiar with it. This shuffle is not difficult, but it will require some practice to perform it smoothly.

METHOD

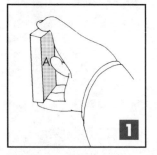

1 Hold the pack in your right hand with your thumb at one end and your second, third, and fourth fingers at the other. The tip of your first finger (bent at the knuckle) should rest against the back of the top card of the pack. The pack should be held so that your right thumb is toward the ceiling with the face of the pack pointing to your left.

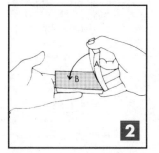

2 Place the palm of your left hand on the bottom of the pack, as shown. With your right hand, bend the pack outward and riffle about half of the pack with your right thumb, allowing the cards to fall forward onto the left fingers.

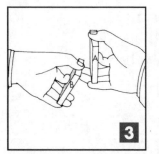

3 Place the tip of your left thumb on the back of this new packet (B) and raise the lower end of Packet B upward until it clears Packet A in the right hand. As the end of Packet B comes clear, shift your left thumb to the right-hand end of Packet B.

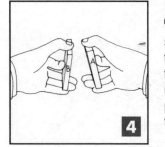

4 The two packets should be facing each other, held with the same grip in each hand. Your thumbs should be at one end of the packets with your first fingers resting against the backs of the packs and the remaining fingers at the opposite ends.

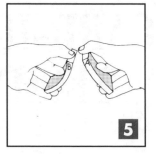

5 Turn both packets face down and move the "thumb end" of each packet together. The backs of the second, third, and little fingers of both hands should rest on the top of the table.

6 Slowly begin releasing (riffling) cards from both thumbs, causing the cards to fall to the table and become interlaced at the inner ends. The ends of the cards should overlap about 1/2" as they are shuffled together.

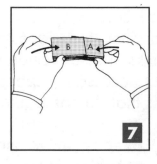

7 When all the cards have been shuffled from both packets, push the two packets completely together and square the deck. This completes the riffle shuffle.

8 Repeat Steps 1 through 7 in quick succession, executing the shuffle as many times as you wish to thoroughly mix the cards.

TABLE SHUFFLE

This basic exercise is intended to show you how to shuffle a deck of cards in the proper manner. This is similar to, but considerably more "professional" than the standard riffle shuffle. When working with cards, it is to your advantage to be able to mix the cards in a quick, graceful fashion. Since some of the best card tricks are performed while seated at a table, you should be familiar with the table shuffle. It gives your work an expert look, convincing your audience that even your simplest tricks are the result of great skill.

EFFECT

You divide the pack into two packets that rest face down on the table. Lifting the rear edges of both packets, you begin to release the cards in succession, causing their corners to interweave as they fall. You push the two packets together and square the deck, thoroughly mixing the pack.

METHOD

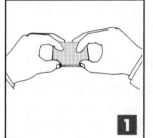

1 Place the pack face down on the table in front of you and grasp the sides of the pack from above, as shown. Using your thumbs, lift about half the pack from the top of the deck, near the middle.

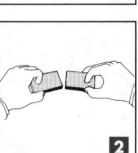

2 Separate the halves and place the packets on the table, as shown. The outer ends of both packets should be angled toward you to bring the innermost corners of the packets very close together. Hold both packets with your thumbs along the inner edge. The first finger of each hand rests on the top of the packs, and the remaining fingers rest along the outer edges.

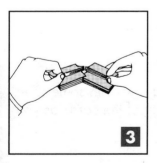

3 Lift the inner edge of both packets with your thumbs and move the packets together so that the innermost corners will overlap slightly. Begin releasing the cards from your thumbs, allowing them to riffle downward onto the table so the inner corners of the cards weave together.

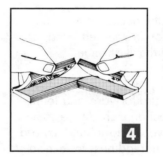

4 The cards are released from your thumbs, interlacing at the corners only, as shown in this close-up view.

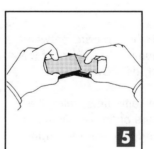

5 Release the remaining cards in the same fashion.

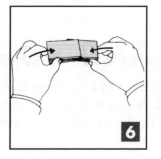

6 Move your fingers to the extreme ends of both packets and push them together to form one pack.

7 Repeat the shuffling process as many times as you like until all the cards in the pack have been completely mixed.

COMMENTS AND SUGGESTIONS

This type of shuffle, sometimes known as the "Dovetail Shuffle," is often used by gamblers or professional dealers. Therefore, it is particularly effective when doing card tricks that have a gambling theme. Many gamblers, after completing the shuffle, will cut the pack by drawing out the lower half of the pack and placing it on top of the upper half of the pack. As a magician, you can follow the same procedure, adding a natural and professional touch to your card work.

DEALING THE CARDS

 Few actions are simpler than dealing cards from the top of the pack, but to do it smoothly, neatly, and sometimes rapidly, the hands should work together, as described here.

METHOD

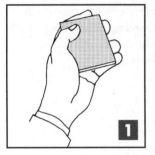

1 Hold the deck in the dealing position in your left hand, as shown in the illustration.

2 With your left thumb, push the top card forward and to the right about an inch. At the same time, move the right hand toward the pack in readiness to receive the card.

3 Grasp the top card between the thumb and fingers of the right hand, as shown.

4 At the same time, relax the pressure of the left thumb on the top card, allowing the right

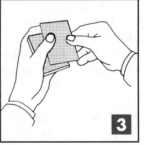

hand to carry the card from the deck to the table.

5 The right hand releases its grip on the card and leaves it on the table. The action can be repeated as often as necessary to deal the appropriate number of cards.

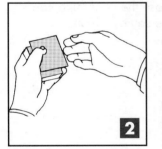

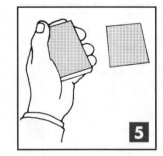

COMMENTS AND SUGGESTIONS

With some tricks, you may deal the cards in a single pile; with others, you may deal them in a row or in some special formation. When dealing cards in a pile, one on top of the other, you will reverse the order of the cards as you deal them. This is known as the "Reverse Deal," an important element in certain tricks.

CHAPTER 2

SELF-WORKING CARD TRICKS

There are many excellent card tricks that practically work themselves and are nearly fool-proof from the magician's point of view, yet really baffle the spectators.

In this section, you'll find some of the best of these self-working mysteries that are both deceptive and easy to perform. You can concentrate almost entirely on the presentation without worrying about any special moves or sleights.

Often, when smart spectators are watching for special moves, you can really flabbergast them with a self-working effect. Make it your policy to include a few self-workers when the occasion demands. You may discover that such effects will be regarded as highlights of your program.

Most importantly, never neglect practice with a self-working trick, even though it seems unnecessary. If you fumble or hesitate, the effect will lose its impact. Always remember that a trick is only as good as you make it look!

DOUBLE TURNOVER

In this card effect, the spectator plays such an active part that trickery seems impossible, yet the magical result is attained while the pack is practically in the spectator's hands. The secret is so simple that once you know it, you can fool an audience the first time you try.

EFFECT

You place a deck of cards on the table and invite a spectator to remove the upper half of the pack, while you take the remaining, lower half. Each of you puts your half behind your back and removes a card at random. Each lays a half pack on the table and looks at the card selected. Then you and the spectator exchange selected cards without looking at each other's cards. You insert the cards face down into the respective half packs—your card in the spectator's half pack and the spectator's card in your half. The full pack is immediately reassembled and both call out the names of the cards each has selected. The pack is spread face down on the table, and both cards have magically turned face up in the deck!

METHOD

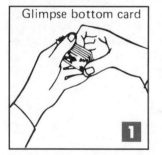

Glimpse bottom card

1 Before the trick, give the pack a few cuts or a shuffle. In the process, casually spot the bottom card of the deck, in this case, the five of hearts, and remember it.

2 Lay the pack on the table and tell the volunteer to cut the pack halfway and hold it behind the back. You do the same with the remaining lower half.

Spectator takes top half

3 Instruct the volunteer to remove any card from the top half of the deck, while you supposedly do the same from the bottom half. Actually, you turn your half face up. Then turn the card you glimpsed, the five of hearts, face down on top of the face-up packet.

4 Also remove any other card from your half. Turn this card face down and bring it out from behind your back. To the spectators, this is the card you selected.

Cards behind magician's back

NOTE: The spectators do not suspect that your actions are different

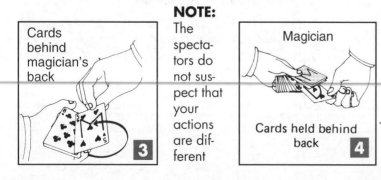

Magician

Cards held behind back

from the volunteer's. In the illustration, your card, the five of hearts, is marked with an "M"; the volunteer's card, in this case, the two of diamonds, is marked with an "X." The random card that you place on the table is marked with a "D" because it is a decoy that plays a special part, as you will see.

5 Tell the volunteer, "Look at the card you drew and remember it, while I do the same with my card." The volunteer looks at the card and notes that it is the two of diamonds. You look at your card, but it is not necessary to remember it—just don't forget your special card, the five of hearts.

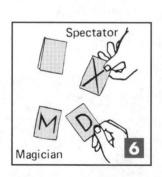

Spectator

Magician

6 You continue, "Hold your card so I cannot see what it is, and lay your half of the pack face down on the table, just as I am doing. Do not tell me what card you selected. I will also keep my card a secret for just a moment."

7 You bring out your half of the pack from behind your back and set it on the table. Your half appears to be the same as the volunteer's half. Actually, all of the cards in your half are face up except for the five of hearts, which is face down at the top.

NOTE: Care must be taken to place the cards on the table squarely so as not to flash any of the face-up cards beneath the five spot.

Cards exchanged

8 You add, "Give me your card, and you take mine, but I won't look at the face of your card, and you don't look at mine. That way, only we will know which cards we took."

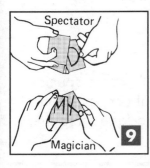

Spectator

Magician

9 With your half of the pack resting on the table, insert the volunteer's card into your half near the center, keeping your half well squared with your left hand. Tell the volunteer to push your card face down into the other half of the pack.

NOTE: At this point, your half of the pack has all its cards face up except for the five of hearts which is face down on top and the volunteer's card, the two of diamonds, which is face down near the middle.

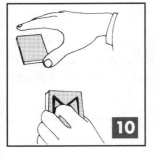

10 Place your left hand over the top of your half in readiness to pick it up from the table. At the same time, with your right hand, reach for the volunteer's half, stating that you will add it to your own.

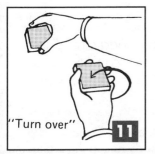

"Turn over"

11 At the exact moment your right hand picks up the volunteer's packet, lift your packet from the table with your left hand and, in the same motion, turn your half over. Your half now really is face down except for the face-up five of hearts on the bottom. This is the only tricky part of this effect. It does not require skill, merely the correct timing. It should be practiced before you present the trick.

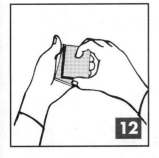

12 Move your hands together and place the volunteer's half on top of your half, squaring the halves together.

13 The entire pack is face down, except for your five of hearts, which is on the bottom, and the volunteer's two of diamonds, about a dozen cards above.

Remove top third of deck and place on table

14 Cut the pack about 1/3 of the way down in the deck and place this packet on the table.

Complete cut on table

1/3   2/3

15 Complete the cut by placing the remainder of the deck on top.

16 As you complete the cut, say to the volunteer, "My card was the five of hearts, what was yours?" Of course, the reply will be, "The two of diamonds." Square the pack and riffle the ends twice with your finger. Say, "Good! Now I'll make both cards magically reveal themselves."

17 Ribbon spread the pack (see page 83) along the table, face down, separating the cards rather widely. As you do, the two cards, the five of hearts and the two of diamonds, are seen to be face up in the spread, providing a startling climax.

COMMENTS AND SUGGESTIONS

When only a few spectators are present, it is not necessary to put the packs behind your back. Instead, you and the volunteer can simply turn away so that neither sees what card the other takes. This gives you an easy opportunity to note a card and place it face up on the bottom, while drawing out another card to serve as a decoy.

In either case, always use a pack with backs that have a white margin around the edges and be sure to keep the cards well squared when handling your half of the pack. Otherwise, a sharp-eyed spectator may notice the face-up cards in your supposedly face-down packet. In turning your left hand over to bring your inverted half of the deck to normal, as shown in Figs. 10 and 11, you can cover the turnover by moving your left hand, with its packet, to the right. This way, you must reach across your left hand with your right in order to pick up the volunteer's packet. That brings your right arm directly over your left hand, allowing you to do the dirty work under cover.

SIGNED CARD IN WALLET

Here is an effect that will cause spectators to give you credit for remarkable skill, yet no special moves or long practice is required. Misdirection is the main factor and even that becomes almost automatic, if you follow this timely, well-paced routine that has been carefully designed to baffle even the sharpest spectators.

EFFECT

A card is selected by a spectator who signs the back of the card. The magician brings out a wallet which contains a prediction card which the magician has signed. When the prediction card is revealed, it is found to match the spectator's selection.

SECRET AND PREPARATION

For this trick, you need a few simple props. First, an ordinary book-style wallet or checkbook. You will also need a pen, a small piece of either double-stick cellophane tape or regular cellophane tape made into a Magic Loop (see page 88) and a deck of cards. In addition, you will need one duplicate card from another deck. It can be any card you choose, but for our explanation, we will use an extra four of hearts. This card, known as the prediction card, can be taken from a pack of a totally different design.

A Open the wallet or checkbook flat and place it on the table, as shown. Next, sign your name across the back of the duplicate four of hearts and place it face down on the left side of the wallet. Fold over the right side, enclosing the card inside the wallet.

C With the taped side toward your body, insert the wallet in your left, inside coat pocket.

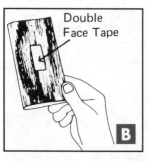

Double Face Tape

B Turn the entire wallet over and place a small (1-1/2") piece of double-stick cellophane tape or a Magic Loop of regular cellophane tape in the center of this side of the wallet. Turn the wallet back over to its original position. Be careful not to stick the tape to the table.

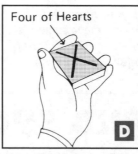

Four of Hearts

D Place the pen in the same pocket. Look through the deck until you locate the four of hearts. (This has been marked with an "X" in the illustrations.) Remove the four and place it on top of the deck. You are ready to perform a truly fantastic trick.

METHOD

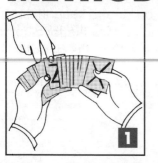

1 Spread the deck face down from hand to hand and ask a spectator to just touch a card. Emphasize that the volunteer has a completely free choice of any card.

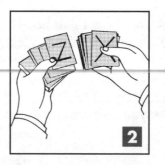

2 When the card has been touched, separate the pack above the card (here marked with a "Z") that the spectator indicated. Keep the selected card (Z) at the top of the left half of the pack.

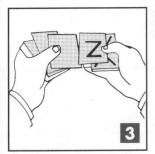

3 Place this selected card (Z), without looking at it, on top of the cards held in the right hand, explaining that you will move the chosen card to the top of the deck.

4 Next, place the right-hand packet of cards on top of those in the left hand and square up the cards. You should now have the selected card (Z) on top of the deck, with the four of hearts (X) directly below it.

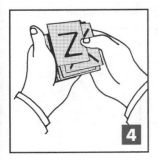

5 Hold the deck in your left hand. With your right hand, bring the wallet from your inside coat pocket. Handle it in a casual manner, keeping the taped side toward you.

6 Tilt the top (upper end) of the wallet toward your body, so the taped side is underneath. With your right hand, place the wallet squarely on top of the pack in the left hand.

7 Hold the wallet against the deck with your left thumb while your right hand moves back toward the pocket for the pen. With your thumb, press firmly on the wallet, causing the top card (Z) to stick to the tape on the underside of the wallet.

8 With your right hand, remove the pen from your pocket and hand it to the spectator.

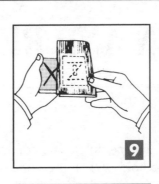

NOTE: Reaching back into your pocket supplies a perfect reason for momentarily leaving the wallet on the deck as a resting place as you bring the pen out to give to the spectator.

9 With your right hand, remove the wallet from the top of the deck to the table, secretly carrying away the spectator's card (Z) with it. The spectator thinks the selected card is still on top of the deck. In fact, the four of hearts is in its place.

10 Deal the top card (now the four of hearts) onto the table, face down, to the left of the wallet. Say, "I'd like you to sign your name across the back of your card to clearly identify your selection."

11 Have the spectator sign the back of the card (really the four of hearts). When the spectator is finished, replace the pen in your coat pocket.

Card with your name

12 Open the wallet to reveal your signed, face-down prediction card. Remove the card from the wallet and place it, still face down, on the table next to the spectator's card.

13 Pick up the wallet and place it back in your coat pocket, thus getting rid of any evidence beforehand. Be sure to handle the wallet so as not to reveal or unstick the card held on the underneath side.

14 Before turning the two cards over, pause a moment to tell your audience about the "mysteries of ESP," thus building up the suspense a little before you turn both signed cards face up. Of course your prediction proves to be correct, making the mystery complete.

COMMENTS AND SUGGESTIONS

This is a very strong mental effect in which no manipulative skill is involved. Present this in your own personal style.

NOTE: Some coats have the inside pocket on the right side, not the left. In that case, after placing the touched card on the top of the pack, transfer the pack from your left hand to your right. Remove the wallet with your left hand and place it on top of the pack in your right hand. The rest of the procedure is exactly the same.

TORN AND RESTORED CARD

EFFECT

A card is selected and signed by the spectator. The card is torn into four quarters. These are wrapped in a handkerchief and given to the spectator to hold. When the handkerchief is opened, all the torn pieces have vanished except for one corner. The magician picks up the deck and riffles it. The selected card jumps out of the deck completely restored, except for the missing corner. The spectator matches the corner to the card and finds that it is a perfect fit!

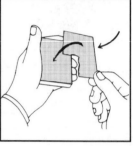

SECRET AND PREPARATION

Before the performance, tear off one index corner of any card. (Discard this corner; you have no further need of it.) Place the torn card face down on top of the deck with the missing quarter at the lower left corner of the deck, as shown. Place another card on top of the torn card to hide it. (The torn-corner card is now the second card from the top of the pack.) Place a small rubber band in your right coat pocket.

METHOD

1 Remove the pack from its case and hold the deck face down in your left hand. Riffle the end of the deck with your right fingers to allow the spectator to select a card. After the card has been removed, immediately place the deck face up on the table.

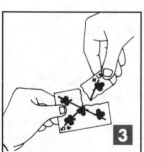

2 As you do this, casually remove the card that is on the bottom of the face up deck. (This is the card that was hiding the torn-corner card.) Gesture with the card as you explain that the spectator could have selected any card. Return this card to the face of the deck.

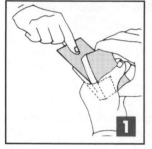

3 Take the spectator's card (X) and tear off one index corner. This should be approximately the same size as the quarter section already torn from the other card.

4 Return the large portion of the chosen card to the spectator and ask the spectator to sign the face of the card. When this has been accomplished, take the card back. Pick up the deck and hold it in your left hand with its face toward the spectators so that they cannot see the other torn-corner card on top. Place the selected card (X) face down on the top of the deck on top of your torn card.

NOTE: The torn corner of the spectator's card is at the upper right-hand corner of the deck (the opposite corner from your previously torn card). The deck may not be lowered or the spectators will be able to see the top.

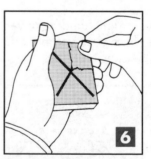

5 Next, ask the spectator to sign the torn corner of the card also. The spectator may use initials or any other identifying mark.

6 While the spectator is doing this, you apparently deal the card face down on the table. Actually, you press your right thumb on the outer right corner of the pack and draw out your card from beneath the selected card.

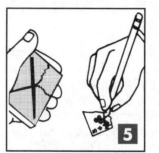

7 This switches your torn card with the selected card, which remains on top of the pack. This move is termed a "second deal." The missing corner of the selected card makes this very easy and deceptive.

8 As you deal the card onto the table, tilt the deck upward, toward your body, so the spectators cannot see the top.

9 With the deck in this position, give the deck one cut to place the selected card (X) in the center of the deck. Lay the deck face down on the table, as you did before.

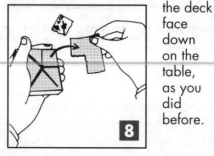

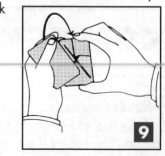

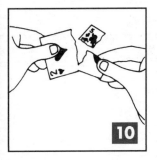

10 Pick up the face-down card, which the audience thinks is the volunteer's signed card, and tear it into three pieces. Keep the pieces turned toward you so that no one can see the face of the card. The audience will suppose that you have torn the selected card into quarters.

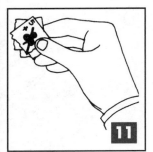

11 Pick up the corner of the selected card (X) and place it on the face of the torn pieces. Hold all the pieces in your right hand. In this way, you can exhibit the pieces, both front and back.

12 Cover the torn pieces held in your right hand with an ordinary handkerchief. With your right thumb, push the corner of the selected card a little higher than the pieces of your card.

13 With your left hand, grasp the corner (X) of the selected card through the fabric. Carry the rest of the torn pieces downward in your right hand, concealing them in the bend of your right fingers. Thrust your right hand into your coat pocket.

14 Leave the pieces in your pocket, bring out the rubber band, and place it around the center of the handkerchief below the marked corner that the audience thinks is all four quarters of the selected card. Give the handkerchief to a spectator to hold and restate what has happened up to this point. Then, add, "Now, for the magic!"

15 Have the spectator remove the rubber band and spread the cloth. Only the torn corner will be found. This will be recognized by the mark or signature made by the spectator.

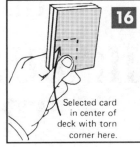

16 Pick up the deck and hold it face down in such a way that the missing portion of the selected card is at the lower left. (The selected card, of course, is buried somewhere in the deck.)

Selected card in center of deck with torn corner here.

17 Riffle the upper right corner of the deck with your right fingertips, keeping the pack tilted upward and forward, while the left hand retains its firm grip.

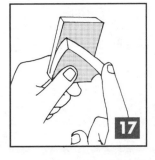

18 The riffle action will cause the selected card (X) to jump halfway out of the deck. This is a very surprising effect, but it is only a prelude to the surprise that follows.

19 Offer this card (X) to the spectator, letting the spectator draw it from the deck. The spectator will be amazed to find that the torn pieces of the card have been magically restored!

20 Have the spectator match the torn corner to this card. It will be a perfect fit. This is the final convincer in a truly great card mystery.

COMMENTS AND SUGGESTIONS

This feat of card magic was originated by the late Paul Le Paul and used for many years. It creates a startling effect that is one of the best in magic. Give this the practice it deserves and you will have a card effect that will entertain and mystify all who witness it.

CHAPTER 3

HINDU SHUFFLE TRICKS

The Hindu shuffle is ideally suited to the needs of present-day magicians, and therefore, is a manipulation that all card workers should acquire. Various factors stand out strongly in its favor. It is easy to learn, it is a legitimate shuffle in its own right, and it is especially suited to card tricks.

As you become familiar with the Hindu shuffle, you will also find that it can be readily adapted to important magical purposes, such as forcing, locating, and controlling desired cards—and all without suspicion on the part of the spectators.

Because of its speed and precision, the Hindu shuffle will give your audience the impression that you are an accomplished performer. That is an important aim when presenting card magic. Some of the simplest tricks can become utterly baffling when the spectators suppose that skilled manipulation is involved.

HINDU SHUFFLE

This type of shuffle supposedly gained its name from the fact that it was occasionally used by Hindu magicians who were unfamiliar with the usual shuffling methods. Whatever its origin, other magicians found that it gave them a great advantage when performing close-up card tricks, as the pack can be handled under the very eyes of the spectators in a deceptive manner without fear of detection. Hence, it is recommended as the first and most important step toward acquiring skill as a card manipulator.

EFFECT

The magician holds a pack of cards in one hand. With the other hand, the magician proceeds to shuffle by repeatedly drawing cards off of the top—from the end of the pack—instead of drawing them sideways as with the overhand shuffle.

METHOD

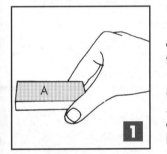

1 Hold the pack face down near one end, with your right thumb and fingers at opposite sides of the pack.

2 Move the pack toward the left hand and grip the top portion of the deck between the tips of the left thumb and fingers.

NOTE: The first finger of the left hand is placed at the end of the pack, as shown. This finger helps to keep the pack squared as you make the following movements.

3 With your right thumb and fingers, draw the bulk of the pack (B) out from beneath as you retain a small block of cards (A) with the fingers of your left hand.

4 As your right hand draws the bulk of the pack (B) clear, release the stack (A) in your left fingers, so that it drops onto the palm of the left hand.

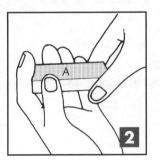

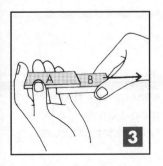

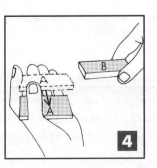

5 Again, move the hands together and grip another small portion of cards from the top of the pack (B) between your left thumb and fingers.

6 Draw the bulk of the pack (C) from beneath the top stack (B).

7 As soon as the pack is clear, let the second stack (B) fall on the first stack (A) already lying in the left hand.

8 Continue drawing off packets into the left hand until the right hand has only a small stack of its own (C), which you simply drop on the pack in the left hand.

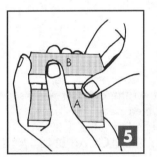

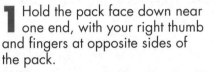

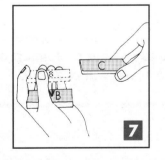

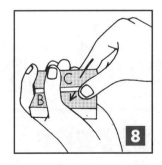

COMMENTS AND SUGGESTIONS

The shuffle should be executed at a moderately rapid pace, keeping the hands in continuous motion as you draw off the packets. This gives a polished and professional look. Because it is adaptable to various uses, the Hindu shuffle is the basis for a whole series of clever, but easy manipulations that will be described as we proceed. You will run into frequent mentions of the basic Hindu shuffle and its more advanced forms throughout this series of lessons.

HOW TO USE HINDU SHUFFLE

 Although the Hindu shuffle actually mixes the pack, it has many magical uses as well. Once you have practiced and learned the regular Hindu shuffle just described, you can use it to accomplish any of the three following purposes. These are indispensable in the presentation of good card magic.

1 LOCATING A SELECTED CARD: A card, freely selected from the pack, is replaced wherever the chooser wishes. Yet, you can find the card in the shuffled deck. This uses a combination of a key card and the Hindu shuffle. (HINDU KEY-CARD LOCATION and SHORT CARD LOCATION.)

2 FORCING A SPECIFIC CARD: A spectator has apparently free choice of any card in the pack, but you force

the spectator to pick the one you want (HINDU FLASH FORCE).

3 CONTROLLING THE LOCATION OF A CHOSEN CARD (OR CARDS): After a card has been replaced in the pack, you can control it to the top or bottom of the deck while giving the deck an honest Hindu shuffle (HINDU SHUFFLE CONTROL).

HINDU GLIMPSE

 The HINDU GLIMPSE is a very useful and valuable move used with the Hindu shuffle. It enables you to see the bottom card of the deck secretly, in a natural manner that even the keenest observer will overlook.

EFFECT

The magician mixes the pack thoroughly, using the regular Hindu shuffle. To keep the pack well-squared during this procedure, the magician taps the inner end of the left-hand packet with the right-hand pack, pushing any protruding cards into place. This very action would seem to the spectators to eliminate the possibility the magician might have of seeing any cards in the pack. Actually, it works to the magician's advantage, enabling the performer to secretly note the bottom card of the right-hand packet.

METHOD

1 Begin with the regular Hindu shuffle, drawing off small blocks of cards from the top of the deck into the left hand.

2 At some point during the shuffle, when you hold about the same number of cards in each hand, turn the right-hand packet at a slant, toward you, and tap the inner end of the left-hand packet in the pretense of squaring up the cards in that hand. This gives you the opportunity to sight the bottom card of the right-hand packet, the two of diamonds.

3 Continue the shuffle, pulling off small packets from the top of the right-hand cards.

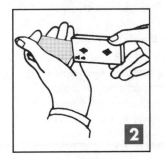

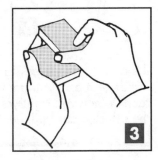

COMMENTS AND SUGGESTIONS

You only need a brief moment to glimpse the bottom card. Just make the move as a natural part of the shuffle. The HINDU GLIMPSE has many magical uses, as you will see.

HINDU KEY-CARD LOCATION

Here is an example of a clever use of the HINDU GLIMPSE.

EFFECT

A spectator freely shuffles the deck as many times as desired and then has a free selection of any card. While the magician gives the deck a Hindu shuffle, the spectator returns the card to the pack at any time. The magician then shuffles the cards and gives them several cuts, yet the magician is still able to find and announce the spectator's selected card.

METHOD

1 Let the spectator freely shuffle the deck as many times as desired so that you cannot know the location of any card.

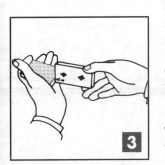

2 Ribbon spread (see page 83) the cards on the table, or just spread them face down in your hands, so the spectator may have a completely free selection. Ask the spectator to pick any card.

3 Gather up the cards and begin the Hindu shuffle. As you do the shuffle, glimpse and remember the bottom card of the packet in your right hand (HINDU GLIMPSE, see page 20), in this case, the two of diamonds. This will be your key card in locating the spectator's card.

Spectator returns card here

"Key" card

4 Tell the spectator to look at the selected card (X) and remember it. Continue to shuffle and tell the spectator to stop you when ready to replace the card.

5 When the spectator says, "Stop," have the spectator return the card (X) to the top of the packet of cards in your left hand.

"Key" Card

6 You immediately drop the cards in your right hand on top of the left-hand packet, burying the spectator's chosen card in the pack. This places the two of diamonds (your key card) directly above the spectator's chosen card (X).

7 Give the deck a few single cuts or let the spectator make the cuts. Turn the deck face up and spread it between your hands. Act as if you are concentrating on the spectator's face. When you sight your key card, the two of diamonds, the selected card (X) will be immediately to its right. After a

suitable period of time, announce the name of the card.

IMPORTANT NOTE: In using the HINDU KEY-CARD LOCATION system just described, you may sometimes encounter a hesitant spectator who does not wish to replace the chosen card until you are about to drop your last few cards on top. That means that you may have to complete the shuffle and begin all over, which is perfectly natural. However, if that happens, your key card becomes lost. Just start the shuffle again and glimpse and remember the new bottom key card.

COMMENTS AND SUGGESTIONS

This is an example of using the HINDU GLIMPSE to get your key card next to the spectator's selected card in a very clever way, even though the spectator has first shuffled the deck.

HINDU FLASH FORCE

There are many ways of forcing a spectator to select a certain card without having the spectator realize it, but to do this naturally and repeatedly was formerly somewhat difficult. It took the Hindu shuffle to produce a surefire way of forcing a card at a moment's notice. Try the method that follows and you will see why.

EFFECT

During the course of a Hindu shuffle, at any time the spectator requests, the magician pauses long enough to give the spectator a "flash" of a card in the pack. Though the magician keeps his own head turned so that he cannot possibly see the card, the magician has actually forced the spectator to select the very card that the magician wanted.

METHOD

1 Suppose you want to force the five of diamonds. Place the five on the bottom of the pack. Start the usual Hindu shuffle, telling the spectator to call, "Stop," at any time.

3 When the spectator says, "Stop," slant the right-hand packet toward the spectator, showing the spectator the face of the card on the bottom. This is the original bottom card of the pack, the five of diamonds!

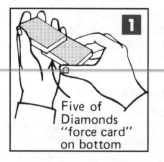

Five of Diamonds "force card" on bottom

2 Continue the shuffle at the usual speed, pulling packets from the top of the cards in the right hand. This leaves the five of diamonds at the bottom of the right-hand cards.

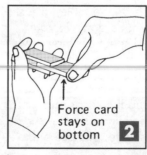

Force card stays on bottom

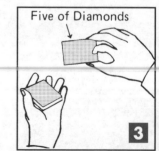

Five of Diamonds

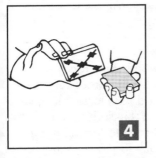

4 Tell the spectator to remember the selected card. (Here is a view as the spectator sees it. Notice that the right hand is well forward toward the spectator to ensure that you cannot see the card on the bottom.)

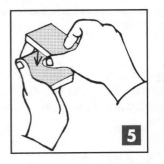

5 Drop the right-hand cards on the cards lying in your left hand to bury the card the spectator thinks was freely chosen from the deck. Actually, you already know the card. You have forced him to select the five of diamonds, just as you had planned!

COMMENTS AND SUGGESTIONS

This is called a "flash force" because you simply flash the card before the spectator's eyes. However, it is more than that. You can hold up the packet as long as you want. Just assure the spectator that you cannot see the card. When the spectator is looking at the card, you should turn your head away to emphasize that you are the one person who cannot possibly see that card. This is important because it diverts the audience from the fact that you don't need to see it, because you already know what it is. This is one important use of misdirection.

COLOR-CHANGING DECKS
TWO-DECK VERSION

In this modified version of the HINDU COLOR CHANGE, you take the mystery one step further by adding a second pack of cards—of a different color—and converting the effect from a color change to a magical transposition of the two packs.

EFFECT

The magician removes a red-backed pack of cards from its case and spreads them face up so that everyone can see that they are all different. Then, running through the face-up pack with a series of short cuts, the magician shows the red backs of the cards at frequent intervals, finally placing the pack face up on the table next to its red box. The performer then follows the exact same procedure with a blue-backed pack of cards, and places it face up on the table next to its blue box. The mystery begins when the magician removes one card from each pack. The one red card is placed on the face of the blue-backed pack, and the one blue card is placed on the red-backed pack. Explaining that this will cause the rest of the cards in both packs to "follow the leader," the magician turns over each pack and spreads it face down next to its correct colored box. The audience is amazed to discover that all the blue-backed cards have magically changed places with all of the red-backed cards!

SECRET AND PREPARATION

The only items required for this mystery are a red-backed pack of cards and its red box and a blue-backed deck and its blue box with a matching design. To prepare, remove a single blue card from the blue pack and place it face down on top of the red deck. Place a single red card on top of the blue deck. Now, place the red deck (with the one blue card on top) into the blue box and place the blue deck (with the one red card on top) into the red box. You are now ready to perform COLOR CHANGING DECKS.

METHOD

1 To begin, place both packs (in their boxes) on the table. Say, "I have two packs of cards, one red and one blue."

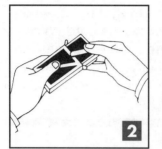

2 Pick up the blue box and remove the pack of cards, face down, so the single blue card, which matches the color of the box, is seen by the spectators. They will assume it to be an all blue pack.

NOTE: As you remove the pack from the box, keep the cards squared so you do not accidentally shift the top blue card exposing the red cards below it.

3 Place the empty blue box on the table and turn the pack over (face up). Run through the pack, showing the faces of the cards. Say, "As you can see, all the cards in the pack are different, as they should be."

4 Square the pack face up in your left hand and begin a regular Hindu shuffle, with the deck face up. At various intervals throughout the shuffle, execute a repeated flash force. The audience believes you are cutting the pack at various places showing a different card each time. Remark, "And the backs are all blue, as they should be."

NOTE: In this trick, the Hindu shuffle must be carried out to the very last card.

5 As you complete the Hindu shuffle, the left fingers draw off all the remaining red cards, leaving the single blue card in your right hand. Finish the shuffle by dropping the blue card on top of the face-up deck.

6 Next, square up the pack and place it face up on the table next to the empty blue box from which you removed it.

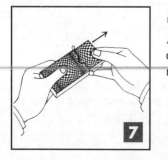

7 Pick up the red box and remove the "red" pack (actually the blue pack with the single red card on top).

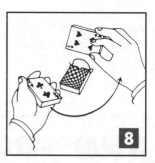

8 Follow the same face-up Hindu shuffle procedure using the repeated flash force, showing the red card. Finish by shuffling the single red card to the top of the face-up pack. Square up this pack and place it face up on the table next to the empty red box.

9 The packs are now resting face up next to their "own" colored boxes.

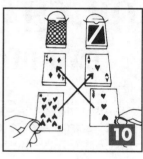

10 Lift the two top cards (the single red card and the single blue card) from the face of each pack and transpose them.

11 Place the red-backed card on the real red pack and the blue-backed card on the real blue pack. As you do this, say, "If I move just one card from each pack and place it on the pack of the opposite color, the rest of the cards in each pack will "follow the leader."

12 Pick up both packs, one in each hand, and spread them face down on the table next to the box you first removed them from. The audience will be amazed to see that the blue cards have magically changed places with the red cards—right before their eyes!

HINDU SHUFFLE
BOTTOM STOCK CONTROL

In certain card tricks, it is important that during a shuffle the bottom card (or a group of cards already on the bottom) is retained there for some future purpose. Here is a way of accomplishing that with the aid of the Hindu shuffle. This is an important utility sleight that every card worker should learn.

EFFECT

To all appearances, the magician gives a pack a regular Hindu shuffle. Yet, in this modified version, the bottom stock of cards remains undisturbed or unshuffled. Despite that important difference, the magician can switch from this form of the Hindu shuffle to another without any chance of detection.

METHOD

1 Hold the pack in the tips of the fingers of the left hand, ready for the Hindu shuffle.

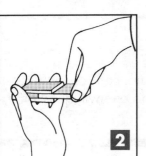

2 Unlike a regular Hindu shuffle, where the right hand begins by drawing off a group of cards from the bottom of the pack, this time the right hand pulls out a section of cards from the center, leaving the bottom group intact. The left hand retains the bottom stock and a small batch of cards from the top as in the usual shuffle.

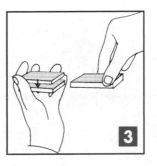

3 Once the right hand has drawn the center packet of cards clear of the bottom and top packets, the left hand allows the top packet to fall onto the bottom packet.

4 Continue the regular Hindu shuffle, repeatedly pulling off small batches of cards from the right-hand pack until the shuffle is complete.

5 The pack has now been fairly shuffled except for the small batch of cards that remains undisturbed. You are also now set to repeat the HINDU SHUFFLE – BOTTOM STOCK CONTROL as often as you like.

FALSE CUT

EFFECT

Many very good card tricks depend on your knowing the bottom card of the pack or bringing a chosen card to the top. At that point, a suspicious spectator may want to cut the pack. So, to prove that all is fair, your best policy is to beat them to it by cutting the pack yourself. You can do that with the following FALSE CUT that looks like the real thing but actually leaves the pack just as it was.

METHOD

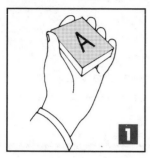

1 Hold the deck in the left hand between the tips of the left fingers and thumb.

2 With the thumb and fingers of your right hand, start to draw out about half the pack (B) from the lower part of the deck.

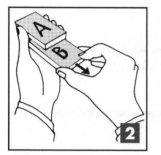

3 As this lower stack (B) comes clear, sweep your right hand toward your body.

4 Continue this sweep, carrying the cards (B) in your right hand up and over the top stack (A) in your left hand.

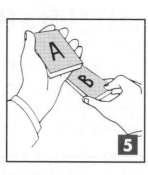

5 Place the packet in your right hand (B) on the table and leave it.

6 With your right hand, take all of the cards (A) from your left hand.

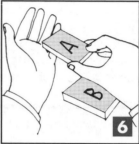

7 Place these cards directly on top of the stack (B) on the table.

8 It will appear as if the cards are fairly cut. Actually, the order of the cards has not changed at all.

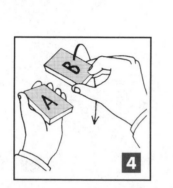

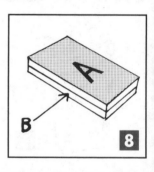

COMMENTS AND SUGGESTIONS

FALSE CUT should be performed at a moderate speed, not too slowly and not too rapidly. Do not call special attention to it, just do it as if you were cutting the cards in a normal manner. If it is done correctly, no one will question it.

HINDU SHUFFLE
PICK-UP CONTROL

This is one of the most deceptive and useful controls in all of card magic. If this sleight were the only one you used with the Hindu shuffle, it would be worth learning it. HINDU SHUFFLE PICK-UP – CONTROL is not difficult to learn. Once you have mastered it, you will be using it in many of your best card effects.

EFFECT

A spectator returns a selected card to the pack while the magician is giving the deck a Hindu shuffle. This apparently loses the card somewhere deep in the pack, yet the magician has secretly controlled the card to the top of the pack.

METHOD

1 Ask a spectator to select a card freely from the pack as you spread the pack between your hands. You can also let the spectator take a card by telling you to "stop" during the course of a Hindu shuffle.

2 While the spectator is looking at the selected card, you square the pack and begin a new Hindu shuffle, inviting the spectator to replace the card at any time. You do the shuffle quite slowly, apparently to aid the replacement, but actually to prepare for a simple but special move.

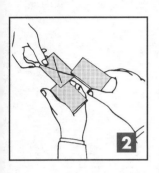

3 After the spectator has replaced the card (X) on the left-hand section of the pack, move the bulk of the pack held in your right hand above the cards in your left hand as if to merely continue the shuffle.

Pick up small packet with right fingers

4 This is the important move. As the left fingers slide off another packet from the top of the bulk of the pack, the tips of your right thumb and second finger squeeze inward, grip the sides, and pick up a small packet of cards from the lower left-hand heap. Carry this small packet away on the bottom of the right-hand bulk of cards. Keep a break or gap between that small batch and the upper bulk of the pack in the right hand.

Selected card on top of small packet

Selected card

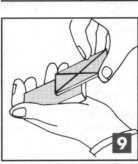

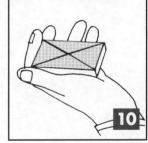

5 The selected card (X) is the top card of this small packet.

6 Continue the shuffle, drawing off cards from the top of the right-hand packet, still holding the small packet on the bottom of the right-hand bulk of cards, always maintaining the gap between the two portions.

7 As you finish the shuffle, the left hand takes all the remaining cards above the gap.

8 At the same time, the right hand draws the little batch out from beneath.

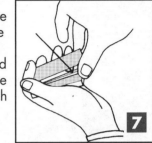

9 The right hand drops the little batch on the left-hand pack to complete the shuffle.

10 Since the chosen card is the top card of the batch, it now becomes the top card of the pack. This means that you have controlled the chosen card to the top of the pack.

COMMENTS AND SUGGESTIONS

The HINDU SHUFFLE – PICK-UP CONTROL is one of the easiest and best ways to bring a selected card to the top of the pack. It also has many other uses and is one of the most valuable sleights you will learn in this book. Study the pictures carefully. The most important move, and the key to this entire sleight, is in Step 4. This is when you pick up the small batch of cards, with the selected card on top, with your right thumb and fingers from the top of the left-hand packet. At the same time that you do this, you pull off a small batch of cards from the top of the right-hand packet, just as if you were continuing the regular Hindu shuffle. This completely covers your secret pick up. You then continue the Hindu shuffle in the normal fashion until you get to the last small batch of cards with the selected card on top. Just place that packet as the last shuffle on the top of the deck in the left hand. Thus, you have secretly brought the selected card to the top. The description of this sleight has been repeated here because of its importance. Once you have mastered the Hindu shuffle and the HINDU SHUFFLE – PICK-UP CONTROL, you have opened the door to hundreds of wonderful, baffling mysteries with cards. If you are interested in performing card tricks, practice and learn this important sleight.

CHAPTER 4
OVERHAND SHUFFLE TRICKS

The overhand shuffle is the most common of all shuffles. The very simplicity of the shuffle makes it easy to locate and control certain cards, bringing them to the top or bottom of the pack and retaining them there.

For that very reason, it should be practiced until it becomes second nature, so that the various subterfuges can be introduced without arousing suspicion. By using the overhand shuffle constantly in card tricks, as well as in card games, you will have a simple opportunity to practice.

Hundreds of excellent tricks can be developed directly from the overhand shuffle, many of which have been included in this book.

OVERHAND SHUFFLE

The overhand shuffle is an honest shuffle. However, it can be adapted to many special uses, such as controlling certain cards without the audience knowing it.

METHOD

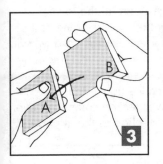

1 Hold the deck with the thumb and fingers of your right hand.

2 Bring both your hands together. With your left thumb, from the top of the deck, pull off a block of several cards (A) into your left hand, leaving the remainder of the deck (B) in the right hand.

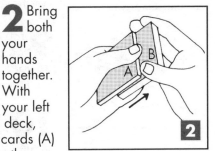

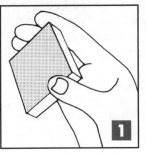

3 Separate your hands completely. Hold the block of cards now in your left hand (A) firmly between the left thumb and fingers.

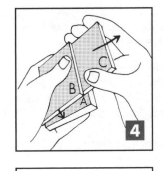

4 Lift your left thumb enough to allow the packet in the right hand to be reinserted into the "pull-off" position. With the left thumb, pull another block of several cards (B) into the left hand on top of the cards (A) already in the hand, leaving the remainder of the deck (C) in your right hand.

5 Separate your hands, allowing the cards just removed (Block B) to fall on the cards already in the left hand (Block A).

6 Continue pulling off blocks of cards until all of the cards in the right hand have been shuffled into the left hand.

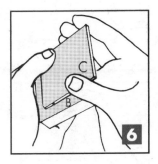

COMMENTS AND SUGGESTIONS

This is a natural way of shuffling a pack of cards and mixing it quite thoroughly, but it can also easily be diverted to magical uses, particularly in controlling cards on either the top or bottom of the pack or to a particular position in the deck. Therefore, easy as this shuffle is, you should practice it repeatedly until it can be executed without hesitation. This will enable you to perform the special variations as required.

OVERHAND REVERSE SHUFFLE

The overhand shuffle can also be done as a reverse shuffle. The movements are exactly the same as described in the overhand shuffle, except that the right hand holds the deck so that the faces of the cards are outward (with the backs of the cards toward the right palm) instead of inward (with the faces of the cards toward the right palm). The operation of the shuffle is the same. However, the reverse has an important bearing on the control shuffles that follow.

OVERHAND IN-JOG CONTROL

METHOD

1 After a spectator has drawn a card from the pack and is looking at it, you start an overhand shuffle, drawing cards from the top of the pack with your left thumb. Tell the spectator to replace the card in the pack as you near the center.

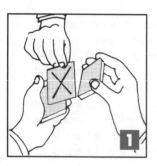

2 The spectator's card goes on the left-hand packet. As you resume the shuffle, bring your right hand slightly inward toward your body, a matter of 1/2" or so. This is a simple action that might occur during any shuffle.

3 With your left thumb, draw off a single card from the right-hand packet. Let this meaningless card fall on the selected card, which is on top of the left-hand packet. The inward movement that you made in Step 2 will make this one card protrude slightly inward, toward your body, from the rest of the left-hand cards.

4 This single, off-center card is called an "in-jog." You can prevent anyone from noticing it by simply moving your right hand forward to its normal position and continuing your overhand shuffle. The remainder of the cards go into their regular position, "evened up" with the first cards shuffled.

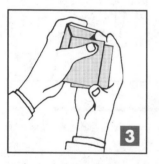

5 As more cards cover the jogged card, they help to hide it from view, particularly if they are shuffled in a somewhat irregular manner.

6 As you continue shuffling off blocks of cards, be sure that the in-jogged card is not pushed back into the deck.

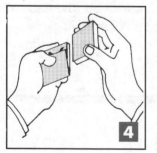

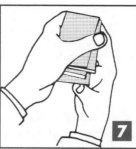

7 Continue shuffling until all the cards from the right hand are held in the left hand.

8 After you have completed the shuffle, the deck should look like this with the jogged card protruding toward you. Of course, since this is a secret maneuver, you do not call the spectator's attention to it.

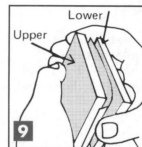

9 You can now easily find the jogged card by pressing upward with your right thumb at the inner end of the pack.

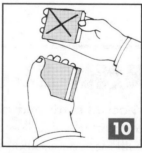

Upper   Lower

10 This upward pressure causes the deck to divide at the jogged card. By gripping the ends of the lower packet between your right thumb and fingers, you can lift the lower portion entirely clear of the rest of the deck. The selected card (X) will be on top of this lower portion.

11 With the right hand, carry the lower section completely over the upper section in the left hand.

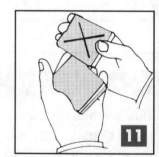

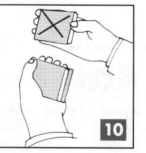

12 Drop the packet in the right hand (with the select card on top) down in front of the cards held in the left hand. This is called a "throw," and to all appearances, it adds a final and convincing touch to the shuffle.

13 Actually, the throw brings the selected card to the top of the pack.

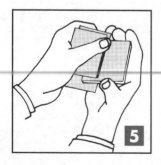

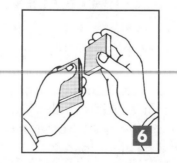

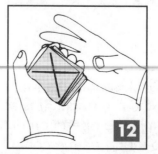

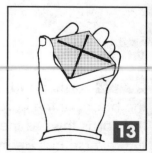

30

COMMENTS AND SUGGESTIONS

Treat the jogged card much as you would any other key card. Never appear to pay any attention to its position, which should be easy, since you are depending on your sense of touch alone. Make the shuffle look natural, even sloppy, if you wish. If your shuffle is too neat, you may lose track of the jogged card. Don't worry if you pull down an extra card or two when making the jog. A little group of jogged cards will function just as effectively as a single card, for when you press the lowest card of the group upward, the others will go along with it, and you will still be able to cut to the selected card and throw the packet to the top of the deck.

CARD CASE ESCAPE

 Variety is an important factor in card tricks that end with the discovery of a card selected by a spectator. Many card discoveries, though clever, are too much alike to be presented in the same program. It is a good idea to inject something distinctly different. This effect will vary your program.

EFFECT

After a card has been selected by a volunteer and shuffled back into the pack, the magician puts the entire pack into its box and closes the flap. Showing the box from all angles, the magician openly places it in a shirt pocket. Then, showing that both hands are empty, the magician reaches into the pocket and instantly removes the chosen card. Immediately, the magician brings the card box from the pocket and gives it to the spectators, allowing the volunteer to open it and examine both box and pack. Apparently, the selected card managed to penetrate the card box under its own power!

METHOD

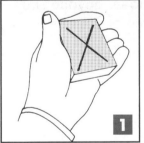

1 Remove a regular pack of cards from its box, shuffle it, and have a volunteer select a card. Tell the volunteer to remember the card and return it to the pack. As the card is returned to the pack, use your favorite method to control it to the top (see pages 30 and 33).

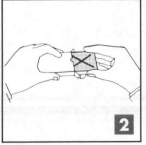

2 Holding the pack in one hand, pick up the card box in the other. Replace the entire pack in the card box, making sure that the top of the pack (with the selected card on it) goes against the side of the box with the little "thumb slot" cut out. As you do this, say, "I will place the pack of cards into its card box, thus sealing your card inside, somewhere in the deck."

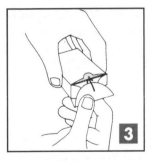

3 Begin to close the lid of the box. As you do, squeeze the sides of the box containing the cards, as shown. This squeezing action will cause the top few cards of the pack to "bow" outward against the top of the box, making a small gap between each of the top few cards.

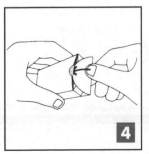

4 As you tuck the flap in, slide it beneath the top card of the pack (the volunteer's card), as shown.

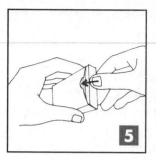

5 Close the flap completely and transfer the box to your right hand.

6 As you hold the case, make sure the fingers of your right hand cover the thumb slot, thus concealing the visible portion of the volunteer's card from view. With the pack held in this manner, you can display it casually on both sides before you proceed to the next step.

7 After briefly showing the box, place it in your shirt or coat breast pocket as you remark, "With the pack sealed in its box and hidden in my pocket, it would be very difficult for me to find your card."

8 Show that your hand is empty and reach into your pocket. Use your fingers to work the end of the volunteer's card out of the box by pulling it from the thumb slot. As soon as you have a good grip on the card, immediately withdraw it from your pocket.

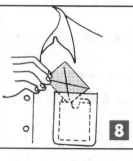

9 The back of the card will be toward the volunteer; therefore, the volunteer will not know what card you have in your hand. Ask the volunteer to name the selected card. When the volunteer replies, turn the card in your hand face up and show it to be the selected card. Immediately remove the pack from your pocket and toss it on the table for all to examine.

COMMENTS AND SUGGESTIONS

The proper type of card case for this trick is one with a flap that slides in easily and rather deeply. Some short flaps will not stay in place while you are extracting the chosen card. As you draw the card from its box, be careful that the flap remains closed. As soon as one hand removes the chosen card from the pocket, the other hand can bring out the case and offer it for examination.

SHUFFLE CONTROL WITH KEY CARD

Whenever you are using a key card to locate a chosen card, you must be careful not to let anyone shuffle the pack, as that may separate the two cards. However, you can do an actual shuffle of your own.

METHOD

1 In Step 6 of the HINDU KEY-CARD LOCATION (see page 21), after you have dropped the upper half of the pack on the lower, placing the key card next to the selected card, begin an overhand shuffle, drawing off little packets of cards from the top of the deck with your left thumb.

Draw off a large packet

2 When you near the center, draw off a large block of cards together. This section contains your two cards, the key card and the selected card. You draw off the large packet of cards so that they will not be separated.

3 Complete the shuffle by drawing off the lower cards in small packets again. You may cut the pack as often as you want.

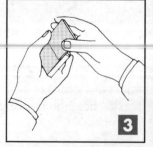

OVERHAND SHUFFLE CONTROL
TOP CARD TO BOTTOM

 With the overhand shuffle, you can control the top card of the pack and bring it to the bottom of the pack while apparently giving the deck an honest shuffle.

METHOD

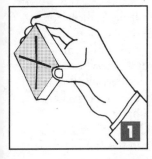

1 Your control card is on the top of the deck. Hold the pack in your right hand.

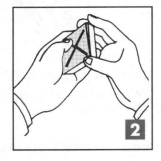

2 Start by drawing off only the top card with the left thumb.

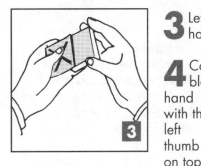

3 Let it fall alone into the left hand.

4 Continue the shuffle, pulling blocks of cards from the right hand with the left thumb on top

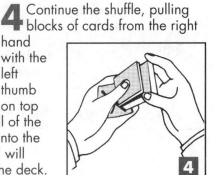

of the control card, until all of the cards have been shuffled into the left hand. The control card will now be on the bottom of the deck.

OVERHAND SHUFFLE CONTROL
BOTTOM CARD TO TOP

EFFECT

In addition to controlling the top card to the bottom of the pack, the OVERHAND SHUFFLE CONTROL (see page 29) can be worked in reverse to bring the bottom card to the top of the pack.

METHOD

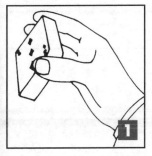

1 Hold the deck face outward as described in OVERHAND REVERSE SHUFFLE (see page 29). Your control card will be the three of diamonds, the bottom card.

2 Turn your body to the left so that the back of your right hand is toward the spectators. This keeps the bottom card out of their sight.

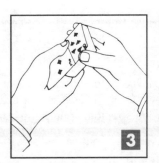

3 With your left thumb, draw off the front card (the three of diamonds) by itself.

4 Continue as already described, shuffling the rest of the deck on top of the three of diamonds. This will bring the bottom card to the top of the pack.

OVERHAND IN-JOG TOP CARD CONTROL

EFFECT

With this control, you perform what appears to be an ordinary overhand shuffle. Yet, when you finish, the top card of the deck is the same card as when you started.

METHOD

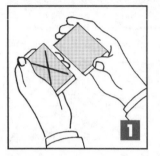

1 The card you will control is on the top of the deck. Start the shuffle by removing a block of cards from the top of the pack with the left hand. The control card is now the top card of this packet.

2 Immediately in-jog the first card you shuffle off from the

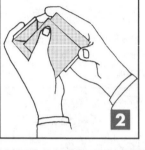

right-hand packet on top of the control card in the left-hand packet.

3 Shuffle off the remainder of the deck in the regular manner, making sure not to disturb the jogged card. After all of the cards have been shuffled into the left hand, cut to the in-jogged card as you did in Step 9 of the OVER-HAND IN-JOG CONTROL (see page 30) and throw the lower packet on top of the other cards in the left hand. The control card will now be back on the top of the pack.

MAGNETIZED CARD

There are many ways in which a magician can discover a card selected by a spectator, but those in which the card actually reveals itself are perhaps the most spectacular. One of the most impressive is the "Rising Card Trick," which has been shown in various forms over a period of many years. Usually, special preparation is needed, but here is a quick and simple impromptu version that can be performed as a close-up mystery with surprising effect!

EFFECT

A card is selected and returned to the pack which is shuffled by the magician in the usual fashion. Holding the pack upright in the left hand, with its face toward the audience, the magician rests the tip of the right first finger on the upper end of the pack. The performer states that the chosen card will be magically magnetized, causing it to rise from the pack of its own accord. As the magician lifts the finger, the card obeys, rising slowly and mysteriously until it is almost clear of the pack.

METHOD

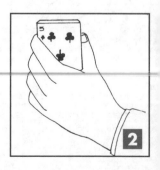

1 From an ordinary pack of cards, invite a spectator to select any card, look at it, and remember it. Using the HINDU SHUFFLE PICK-UP CONTROL (see page 26), or the OVERHAND IN-JOG TOP CARD CONTROL (see above), have the spectator return the card, which you then control to the top of the pack.

2 Hold the pack upright in your left hand with the thumb at one side and the fingers on the other side. The bottom card of the pack should face toward the palm of your left hand, and the back of your left hand should face the audience.

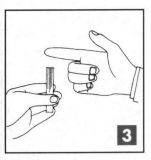

3 With the pack held firmly in this position, extend the first finger of the right hand, pointing it toward the audience. The remaining fingers should be curled into the palm of the hand. Hold your right hand about 6" above the top edge of the pack.

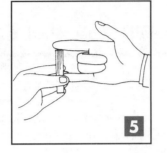

4 Slowly lower your right hand until the tip of the first finger rests on top of the pack, as shown. Continue this up and down motion a few times as you say, "I will now attempt to magnetize the chosen card with my finger and cause it to rise from the pack on its own. Watch closely!"

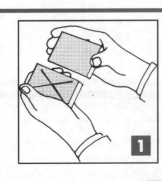

5 With that, lower the right hand until the first finger touches the top of the pack. When it

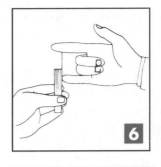

does, straighten out your little finger so it touches the back of the spectator's card, as shown. Because the spectator sees the pack from the front, the extended little finger will not be seen, as it is hidden by the pack.

6 Without hesitation, slowly move the right hand upward as you apply a slight pressure on the back of the spectator's card with the tip of the little finger. This will cause the top card to slide upward and appear to be clinging to the tip of your right forefinger.

7 As the card slides upward, the tips of your left thumb and fingers serve as a guide or track for the card during its rise.

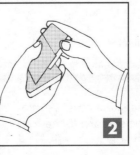

8 When the card has risen almost to the top of the pack, move your right hand away. Let the left thumb and fingers hold the card securely for a moment before removing it with your right hand and tossing it out for inspection.

COMMENTS AND SUGGESTIONS

The important factor in this trick is to guard against bad angles. If your audience is spread out, stand well back so that everyone will have a front view of the deck and be unable to see your little finger extended behind the pack. For close-up work, when performing for just one person, you can hold the pack right before the spectator's eyes, giving your viewer no chance at all to see past the edges.

OVERHAND IN-JOG CONTROL
PLACING A CARD AT A SPECIFIC LOCATION IN THE DECK

EFFECT

This control is very useful in placing a selected card any number of cards down in the pack that you wish. Let's assume that for a particular trick you need the card to be fourth from the top.

METHOD

1 With the selected card on top of the pack, begin a regular overhand shuffle, drawing about half of the top of the pack into your left hand.

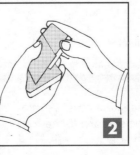

2 One at a time, shuffle off three cards on top of the selected card. Do not jog these cards.

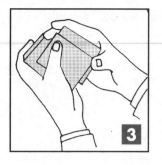

3 In-jog the fourth card and shuffle the rest of the cards on top of it into the left hand.

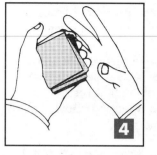

4 Cut the lower portion of the pack at the jogged card and throw the lower block of cards to the top of the deck. The selected card will now be fourth from the top.

SURPRISE APPEARANCE

This is a quick and clever card discovery using the control just described.

EFFECT

The magician has the spectator select a card from the deck and then return it while the magician is doing an overhand shuffle. The magician states that the selected card will be brought to the top of the deck. After the magician fails three times, the selected card makes a surprise appearance.

METHOD

1 Have a card selected and then use the OVERHAND IN-JOG CONTROL (see page 30) to bring the selected card to the top. Using the OVERHAND SHUFFLE CONTROL TO A SPECIFIC LOCATION IN THE DECK just described, control the spectator's card so that it is fourth from the top of the deck.

2 Give the deck a FALSE CUT (see page 25) as previously described.

3 Hold the deck in your left hand and state, "I will now bring your card to the top of the deck." Slap the deck with your right hand and show the spectator the top card.

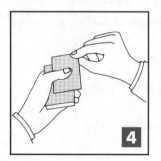

4 When you remove the top card to show it, just slide the card over to the right with your left thumb and then grasp the outer right corner of the card with your right thumb underneath and right first finger on top. Turn the card over, as shown, toward the spectator, so that it is face up.

5 Ask the spectator if this is the selected card. Of course, the reply will be, "No." Replace this card on the bottom of the deck.

6 Slap the deck again and show the next card. Again, you have failed to bring the selected card to the top. Replace this card on the bottom of the deck as well.

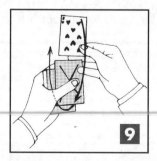

your two fingers for a SURPRISE APPEARANCE.

7 Each time you show a "wrong" card, hold it with your right thumb and first finger and have your hand close to the top of the deck, as shown.

8 As you show the third "wrong" card, push the top card of the pack, which is now the selected card (X), over slightly to the right.

9 As you display your third "mistake," grip the corner of the top card (X) between the tips of the third and little finger of your right hand.

10 Replace the third card on the top of the deck. At the same time, retain your hold on the selected card (X) with your right thumb and little fingers. The selected card (X) will pop up unexpectedly, facing the spectators, held between

Eight of Hearts

CHAPTER 5

FORCING
A CARD

Forcing a card on an unsuspecting spectator is a sure way of bringing a trick to a successful conclusion. Since you already know what card will be chosen before you start, you can finish the trick almost any way you want—and the more surprising, the better. Try the methods given in this section, and you will realize how effective they can be.

It is a good policy to vary your forcing methods so that spectators will not become too familiar with your procedure.

With most tricks, it is best to use a regular card location to reveal a chosen card, reserving the force for times when it is definitely needed. One such time is when a skeptical spectator wants to snatch the pack from your hands and shuffle it until you can't possibly find the chosen card. If you force a card on such a customer, you won't have to worry about this shuffle.

SLIP FORCE – FIRST METHOD

When you want a sure, deceptive force, using any pack of cards, this is one of the very best.

EFFECT

After shuffling a pack of cards, the magician holds the deck face down in the left hand. With the left thumb, the magician riffles the outer corner of the pack downwards. To a spectator, the magician says, "As I riffle the cards, please tell me when you want me to stop."

When the call comes, the magician grips the top portion of the pack in the right hand. Then, lifting that part of the pack upward, the magician extends the bottom portion in the left hand, so that the spectator can look at the top card of that packet—the place where the magician stopped. Apparently, this is a completely free selection, yet the card has actually been forced, thanks to the slip.

SECRET AND PREPARATION

The top card of the deck is the one that is forced. So, you must know the top card beforehand. To do this, glimpse the bottom card using the HINDU GLIMPSE (see page 20). Then, shuffle the bottom card to the top, using the OVER-HAND SHUFFLE CONTROL – BOTTOM CARD TO TOP (see page 33). Begin once the top card is known. (Instead of forcing a particular card, position the card on top of the pack before the spectator makes the free selection.)

METHOD

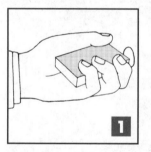

1 Begin by holding the deck in your left hand using the mechanic's grip dealing position: your left thumb is at one side of the pack, your first finger is at the front edge, and the other three fingers are curled over the top of the pack at the right side. (In the illustrations, the force card is marked with an "X.")

2 With your left thumb, bend the outer left corner of the pack downward. Slowly begin releasing cards from the tip of the thumb, allowing them to spring upward, as shown. This is called riffling the cards. As you do this, ask the spectator to call "Stop" at any time during the riffle. Tell the spectator to take the card at the point where you are stopped.

3 Slowly begin riffling the cards. When the call comes, you stop. Without hesitation, move your right hand over the pack and grasp the upper packet of cards (above the point where you stopped) between your right thumb and fingers, as

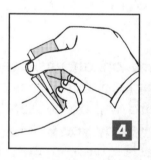

shown. Note that your left fingers are curled over the top card of the pack (X).

4 Begin drawing the top packet upward. The left fingers maintain a downward pressure on the top card (X).

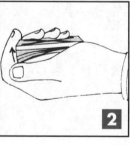

5 Hold the top card (the force card) in place with your left fingers as your right hand slides the top packet from beneath it.

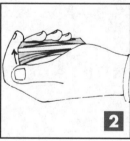

6 The right hand continues to slide out the top packet until it clears the edges of the slipped force card (X), which falls on top of the left-hand packet.

7 Offer the left-hand packet to the spectator. Have them remove the top card, which is now the force card (X), and look at it. You have successfully forced the card on the spectator using the SLIP FORCE. Reveal the name of the card in any manner you choose.

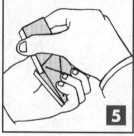

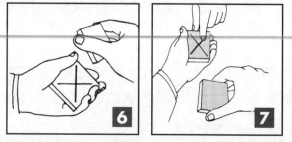

COMMENTS AND SUGGESTIONS

The great feature of the SLIP FORCE is that it is absolutely undetectable when properly handled. As long as the back of your right hand is toward the spectators, the slip will be completely hidden. The same applies when the left hand tilts the pack upward, with the bottom turned toward the audience. (SLIP FORCE – SECOND METHOD, see below.) That is the very reason why you should get it exactly right. In your regular cuts, handle the pack as though you were about to do the slip, then there will be no suspicion when the time comes to actually execute the SLIP FORCE.

SLIP FORCE – SECOND METHOD

The SLIP FORCE is one of the most useful and deceptive methods of having a spectator select a forced card. After you have learned the basic method just described, try this variation which can make the trick even more effective.

METHOD

1 As in the initial description of the SLIP FORCE (see page 38), the top card (indicated by an "X") is the card that will be forced. Follow Steps 1 through 5, just as described in the SLIP FORCE.

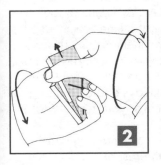

2 When you get to Step 6, the right hand is sliding out the top packet as the fingers of the left hand hold the top card of that packet, which will fall on top of the left-hand packet. At the same time this action is being executed, both hands turn their packets face up. The hands rotate in opposite directions, as indicated by the arrows.

3 Turning the hands over as you make the slip hides the move completely from the spectator's view, even if you are completely surrounded.

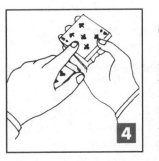

4 At this point, the right-hand packet is face up and the left-hand packet is also face up with the "X" card on the bottom. Extend your left forefinger and point to the card on the face of the right-hand packet. Say, "I don't want you to take this card because I know what it is."

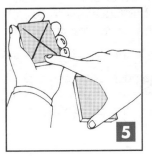

5 With that, turn both hands over, back to their original position. Extend your right forefinger, pointing to the top card of the left-hand packet. Say, "Instead, take this one where you said, 'Stop.'"

COMMENTS AND SUGGESTIONS

As stated above, this variation should be learned after you master the "regular" SLIP FORCE. When you can perform the first method with ease, you can then add this "extra" touch which makes the SLIP FORCE totally undetectable under all conditions.

10–20 COUNT FORCE

EFFECT

The performer asks a spectator to call out any number between 10 and 20, stating that the number that is called is the number of cards that will be counted out from the pack onto the table. This done, the magician then adds the two digits of the selected number together to arrive at a total. The magician counts that many cards from the top of the already dealt pile to arrive at a single card. The spectator is asked to look at that card and remember it. The performer automatically knows the name of this card which was really forced. The magician may now reveal the card in any manner desired.

Tenth card

SECRET AND PREPARATION

Because of a simple but clever mathematical principle, this force actually works itself. The only preparation necessary is that you know the tenth card from the top of the deck beforehand. (In the illustrations, this card is marked with an "X.")

METHOD

1 Hold the deck face down in dealing position in your left hand. Ask the spectator to name any number between 10 and 20. Suppose the spectator says, "13." Count off 13 cards, one at a time, face down in a pile on the table, as shown. This dealing action reverses the order of the cards on the table. This places the force card fourth from the top in your new pile.

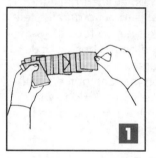

2 Lay the pack aside and pick up the new pile of 13 cards in dealing position. State that you will add the figures of the chosen number "13" (1 + 3 = 4) and count down that many in the pile.

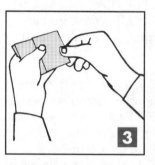

3 You do this with the following result: When you counted the original 13 cards in a pile, you reversed their order as already stated. Now, by counting four cards, one at a time, from that pile, you reverse them again. This system, which works with any number between 10 and 20, causes the count to always end on the original tenth card, your force card!

4 Place the remaining cards with the rest of the deck and ask the spectator to look at the top card of the pile of four and remember it. You have now successfully forced a card using the 10–20 COUNT FORCE. You may reveal the selected card in whatever manner you choose.

COMMENTS AND SUGGESTIONS

The subtle mathematical principle that causes this effect to work can be easily understood by sitting down with the pack and trying out the various number combinations a few times. No matter what number the spectator selects (between 10 and 20), the result is always the same. The original tenth card from the top of the deck always ends up as the selected card.

ROLLOVER FORCE

Here is a surefire method of forcing a card where the actual handling of the pack seems so haphazard and disorderly that it appears impossible for the magician to have control over the position of any card in the pack. This makes for a very convincing force which is ideal for any card worker's program.

SECRET AND PREPARATION

For the ROLLOVER FORCE, all you need is an ordinary pack of cards with the force card on top. (In the illustrations, the force card is marked with an "X.")

METHOD

1 Hold the pack face down, in dealing position, in your left hand. State that you wish to have one card selected from the pack at random. To make sure that this choice is not influenced by you, the magician, you will let the pack itself determine which card will be selected.

2 With that, you lift off the upper 1/4 of the pack (about 10 to 15 cards).

3 Turn these cards over, face up.

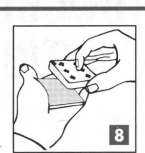

4 Replace them on top of the face-down pack, as shown. As you turn the packet over, say, "To completely confuse the order of the pack, I will not only mix the cards, I'll turn some face up and some face down."

5 To make things more confusing, lift off nearly half the deck (20 to 25 cards).

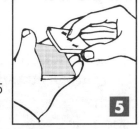

6 Turn these over as before.

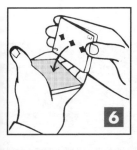

7 Replace these cards on top of the rest of the pack.

8 To add to all this, lift off another stack of cards, this time cutting closer to the bottom (about 3/4 of the deck).

9 Turn these cards over.

10 Replace them on top of the remaining cards.

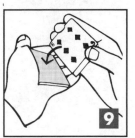

11, 12, 13 You then state, "To confuse matters even further, I'll turn the whole pack over," – which you do.

14 After turning the pack over, say, "Now, we'll run through the pack and take the first face-down card that comes along." With that, you start to spread the pack, "running" the cards from your left hand to your right.

15 The first face down-card you reach will be the force card, the three of clubs. The audience thinks it is just a random card. Have a spectator remove that card from the pack and look at it. When that is done, you have successfully forced the card, using the ROLLOVER FORCE.

CHAPTER 6

DOUBLE LIFT TRICKS

Holding two cards together and exhibiting them as one is perhaps the oldest artifice in card magic. It has attained new value in the comparatively modern sleight known as the DOUBLE LIFT. This maneuver is utterly deceptive in the hands of experts (many of whom have their own pet twist), but the basic principle is the same in all versions.

The DOUBLE LIFT is an effective and useful sleight, providing it is not used too often or too boldly. Originally intended simply to cause one card to "change" into another, newer and more subtle uses for the DOUBLE LIFT were soon devised. You will find a nice variety in this section. The DOUBLE LIFT is most effective when worked in conjunction with other moves. Results can be achieved that seem impossible—and all with an ordinary pack of cards.

LITTLE FINGER BREAK

This secret move is very important. The LITTLE FINGER BREAK has many uses. One of the most useful is to prepare for the DOUBLE LIFT (see page 44).

METHOD

1 Hold the deck in your left hand in dealing position. However, unlike the regular dealing position (A), where the second and third fingers curl over the top of the deck, hold the deck so that just the tips of these three fingers extend above the right edge of the deck (B).

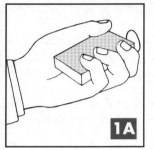

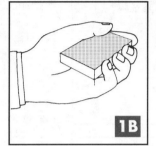

2 Bring your right hand over the deck, right thumb at the inner end, your right first finger resting on top of the deck, and your remaining fingers at the far end of the pack, as shown.

3 With the ball of your right thumb, slightly raise the inner end of the top card off the top of the deck.

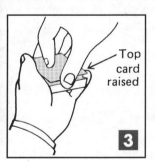

Top card raised

4 In the same motion, bend your right thumb inward just enough to catch the edge of the second card (the one just below the top card) and raise it also just slightly off the top of the deck as well.

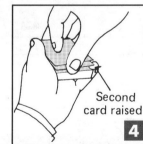

Second card raised

NOTE: The right first finger should apply a slight downward pressure on the top of the deck nearest the audience to assure that only the inner ends of the cards are raised. From the audience's view, it should appear that you are just holding the deck with both hands.

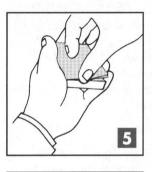

5 When both cards are raised off the inner end of the deck, press lightly against the right side of the deck with your left little finger. This will cause the skin on the ball of the little finger to overlap the top edge of the deck just enough to hold a small break between the two raised cards and the rest of the cards in the deck.

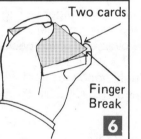

Two cards

Finger Break

6 Relax your right thumb, allowing the two lifted cards to come to rest together on the fleshy tip of your left little finger. You have now secured a LITTLE FINGER BREAK beneath the top two cards.

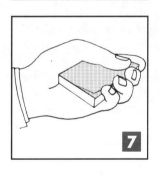

7 Move the right hand away and, at the same time, move the left thumb so that it rests on top of the pack with your left first finger curled around the front of the pack. Keep the "audience end" of the top two cards flush with the deck. The pack, from the audience's view, should look completely natural.

COMMENTS AND SUGGESTIONS

The entire procedure of securing the LITTLE FINGER BREAK should be done deliberately in the pretense of squaring up the deck as it is held in the left hand.

NOTE: It is also important, after you learn the sleight, not to look at the pack as you make the break. This is an example of misdirection, because the audience will look where you look. Make some comment and look at the spectators when you make the secret move.

DOUBLE LIFT

Once you have mastered the LITTLE FINGER BREAK (see page 43) to the point where you can execute the move quickly and without arousing suspicion, you are ready to learn the DOUBLE LIFT. This multi-purpose sleight is one of the most deceptive and practical moves in card magic. It has many uses. Learn it well, as it will soon become the basis for many of your most baffling card mysteries.

METHOD

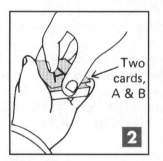

1 As mentioned earlier, you must first learn the LITTLE FINGER BREAK before you learn the DOUBLE LIFT. To execute the DOUBLE LIFT, first secure a LITTLE FINGER BREAK beneath the top two cards of the pack. (These two cards have been marked "A" and "B" in the illustrations.)

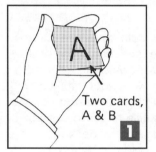

2 Bring your right hand over the pack with your thumb at the inner end, your first finger resting lightly on top, and your other fingers at the outer end of the pack, as shown. This is the same position your right hand was in after securing the LITTLE FINGER BREAK.

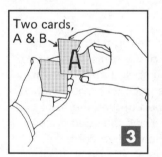

3 With the ball of your right thumb, raise the inner end of the two cards (A and B) you hold above the break. With your right hand, lift both cards together (as one) completely off the top of the pack. Your right first finger should press lightly against the back of the cards. This keeps them from "bowing" apart and holds their edges squared so the two cards appear to be one card.

4 Turn your right hand over, showing the face of the card.

NOTE: The audience believes you have simply picked up the top card of the pack and shown them the face of that card. Actually, the face of the card they see is that of the second card, thanks to the DOUBLE LIFT.

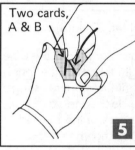

5 Replace the cards back on top of the pack. Be sure that the two cards are squared with the rest of the cards in the pack.

6 With the left thumb, deal the real top card (A) off the pack where it is taken by your right fingers.

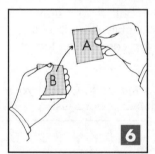

7 Set the pack on the table and turn this card face up, to show that the top card of the pack has magically changed to a different card!

COMMENTS AND SUGGESTIONS

Magically changing the top card into another card is only one of the countless uses of the DOUBLE LIFT. In fact, one of the dangers of the DOUBLE LIFT is that it is so effective, you may be tempted to use it too much. Don't worry about that right now. Just practice and learn this sleight well. As you will see, it will be of tremendous value to you.

RIFFLE REVELATION

♣ This basic application of the DOUBLE LIFT (see page 44) provides a very surprising discovery of a selected card. It can be presented at any time during your regular card routine.

EFFECT

A card is selected and shuffled back into the pack. The performer then shows that the selected card is not the bottom card or the top card, so it must be buried somewhere in the middle. The magician hands the chooser the top card, telling this person to push the card into the pack face down, while the pack is being riffled. Presumably, this card will find the chosen card, but it doesn't. The magician tries again and fails once more. In desperation, the magician looks through the faces of the cards, wondering what could possibly have gone wrong. The magician asks the spectator what card was chosen. When the spectator replies, the magician says, "Well, that explains why we couldn't find your card in the deck. It's the one you had in your hand all the time." To everyone's surprise, the card the spectator holds has magically changed into the selected card!

METHOD

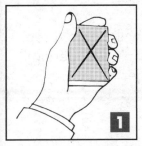

1 From an ordinary pack of cards, have one card selected and returned to the deck. Using any of the methods you have learned (HINDU SHUFFLE PICK-UP CONTROL [see page 26], OVERHAND IN-JOG CARD CONTROL [see page 34], etc.) bring the selected card (X) to the top of the deck.

2 With the chosen card (X) on the top, grip the deck between the right fingers and thumb and turn the entire pack face up, calling the spectator's attention to the card at the bottom of the deck. Say, "There's only a small chance that your card would be the bottom card of the pack. Is this it?" The spectator will answer, "No."

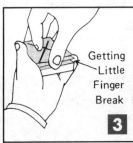

Getting Little Finger Break

3 Turn the pack over and hold it in your left hand in position to execute a DOUBLE LIFT (see page 44). However, before letting go of the cards with the right hand, secure a LITTLE FINGER BREAK (see page 43) beneath the top two cards of the deck.

4 DOUBLE LIFT the top two cards as one card with the right hand. Turn the cards face up, calling attention to what the spectator believes to be the top card of the deck. Ask, "And is this your card at the top of the deck?" Again, the spectator will answer, "No."

5 Replace the two cards on top of the pack. With your right hand, take the top card (X) and hand it, face down, to the spectator. Say, "With the aid of the top card, we will find the exact location of your card in the deck."

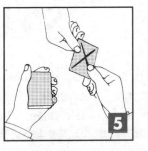

6 Riffle the outer end of the pack with your right fingers. Explain that as you riffle the deck, the spectator is to insert the end of the card into the pack anywhere desired. Tell the spectator that when this is done, the exact spot in the deck where the selected card lies will be found.

7 Here is a side view as the spectator inserts the supposedly meaningless card (really the selected card) into the deck as you riffle. Be careful not to let the spectator see the face of the card and be sure the card is not released. Say, "Just hold onto it firmly."

8 After you have riffled the end of the pack, and the card has been inserted into the deck by the spectator, lift all the cards above the inserted card and turn this packet face up in your right hand to show the card at that point. Inform the spectator that the card on the face of the right-hand packet should be the selected card. But it isn't.

9 Remind the spectator to maintain a hold at all times on what is believed to be a meaningless card (actually, the card the spectator holds is the chosen card).

10 Reassemble the deck and riffle the cards again, explaining that you will give the spectator a second try at finding the card. When you are wrong again, act as if the trick has failed and you don't know why. Turn the cards face up and run through them, as if trying to find the spectator's card.

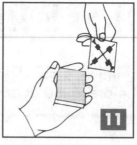

11 Again, still puzzled at your failure, and without looking up from the cards, ask the spectator, "What card did you take?" When the spectator replies, say, "Well, that explains it. You were holding the card all the time." Of course, when the spectator looks, everyone will be surprised that the card has changed in the spectator's hand, while the spectator had control of it all along!

COMMENTS AND SUGGESTIONS

This is a good trick to use when a chosen card is actually found by inserting another in the pack. When people want to see it again, you can use another card instead.

SNAP-IT!

◆ This quick way of magically changing one card into an entirely different card will create a real surprise when injected into a regular card routine. It is guaranteed to keep people wondering what will happen next. This is a classic utilization of the DOUBLE LIFT (see page 44).

EFFECT

The magician removes the top card of the pack and shows it to be the eight of hearts. Turning the card face down, the magician gives it a "snap" with a finger. When the card is turned over, it is seen to have magically changed to an entirely different card!

METHOD

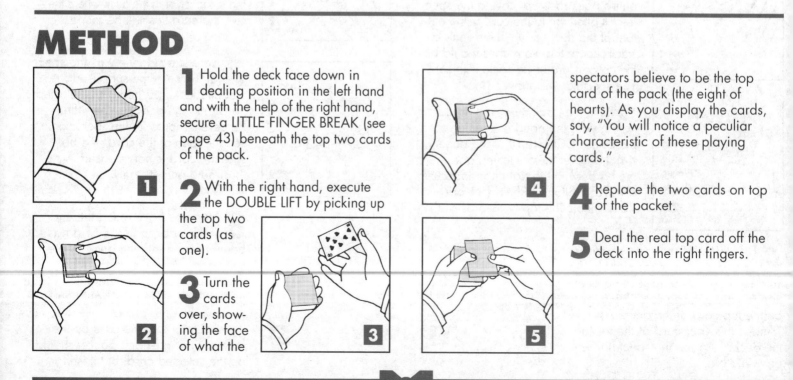

1 Hold the deck face down in dealing position in the left hand and with the help of the right hand, secure a LITTLE FINGER BREAK (see page 43) beneath the top two cards of the pack.

2 With the right hand, execute the DOUBLE LIFT by picking up the top two cards (as one).

3 Turn the cards over, showing the face of what the

spectators believe to be the top card of the pack (the eight of hearts). As you display the cards, say, "You will notice a peculiar characteristic of these playing cards."

4 Replace the two cards on top of the packet.

5 Deal the real top card off the deck into the right fingers.

6 Place the rest of the deck aside. Continue by saying, "If I take the top card of the pack, in this case the eight of hearts, and give it a snap..."

7 Holding the card firmly in the right hand, give the back of the face-down card a sharp snap by hitting it with your left fingers.

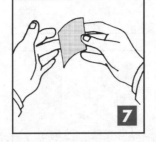

8 Say, "...it causes the card to change, like this!" Turn the card face up.

9 The card has changed from the eight of hearts to the four of clubs!

10 Toss the card on the table, just in case a suspicious spectator should want to examine it—and chances are someone will!

COMMENTS AND SUGGESTIONS

Instead of the change as just described, you can add a clever twist by secretly placing two cards of the same suit on the pack with the lesser value card on top. For example, you might use the four of diamonds on top of the pack with the five of diamonds just below it. Execute the DOUBLE LIFT, replace the cards on the deck, remove the single top card, and hold it in your right hand. Pretend to "knock" one of the spots off the card by snapping it. This can also be done with any two cards of the same suit, just remember to "knock off" enough spots to correspond to the difference in the values of the two cards. If you're working standing up, and have no place to lay the deck aside, simply strike the single card against the pack to "knock off" the spots.

COLOR CHANGING ACES NO. 1

This is a novel and baffling version of the ever-popular FOUR ACES that can be presented in a quick, effective form, ending with a real surprise. In many FOUR ACES routines, extra cards are used, but here, only the four aces are involved, making the entire trick clean, simple, and most startling. The only sleight necessary for this trick is the DOUBLE LIFT (see page 44).

EFFECT

The magician displays the four aces. Holding them in the left hand, the magician deals the two red aces, one at a time, face down on the table. To avoid any confusion, the magician openly shows the face of each red ace before dealing it. This automatically leaves the magician holding the two black aces. At the magician's command, the aces instantly change places. The spectators can even turn over the cards themselves, to find that the black aces are now the two cards on the table and that the magician holds the pair of red aces!

METHOD

1 From an ordinary pack of cards, remove the four aces and place the rest of the pack aside. Display the four aces to the spectators.

2 Arrange the aces in the following order: one black ace on top of the packet (ace of clubs), the two red aces in

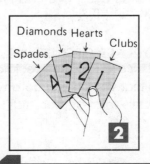

the middle (ace of hearts and ace of diamonds), and the other black ace (ace of spades) at the bottom of the pile. This should be done casually without calling attention to the fact that the cards are in any specific order. (In the illustrations, the aces have been numbered 1 through 4 to make them easier to follow.)

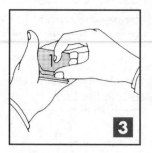

3 With your right hand, place the fanned packet of cards (in their proper sequence) into your left hand, and as you close the fan, secure a LITTLE FINGER BREAK (see page 43) beneath the top two aces (the ace of clubs and the ace of hearts).

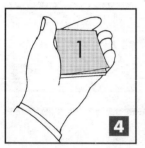

4 You are now ready for the DOUBLE LIFT.

5 Lift the two cards together (DOUBLE LIFT) off the packet and show the face of what the spectators believe to be the top card, the ace of hearts, as you say, "Here is the ace of hearts, a red card, on top."

6 Replace the two cards on the packet and then deal the real top card, the ace of clubs, from the top of the packet to the table as you state, "I will place the first red ace on the table."

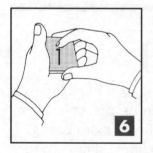

7 This next step is very important. Reverse count the remaining three aces, one at a time, from the left hand into the right hand, as you say, "That leaves one, two, three remaining aces."

8 The reverse count moves the two red aces to the bottom of the packet and the remaining black ace, the ace of spades, to the top.

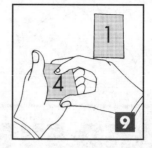

9 Place the packet face down in your left hand as before and, as you square the cards, secure a LITTLE FINGER BREAK beneath the top two cards, the ace of spades and the ace of diamonds.

10 Lift these two cards as one (DOUBLE LIFT) off the packet and show the face of what the spectators believe to be the top card, the ace of diamonds, as you say, "Here is the ace of diamonds, the other red card."

11 Replace the two cards on the packet and deal the real top card, the ace of spades, from the top of the packet next to the ace of clubs already on the table as you say, "The second red ace goes on the table with the first."

12 The rest of the trick is just presentation. After a little byplay, turn over the red aces in your hand and invite a spectator to turn over the black aces on the table to prove that the aces have actually changed places!

COMMENTS AND SUGGESTIONS

By handling the cards in an apparently casual manner, this trick can be built into an extremely deceptive mystery. Here is another clever procedure you can use when you do make the "set-up." After you have opened and removed the aces from the pack and displayed them to the audience, hold them so that only you can see the faces as you arrange the aces in their proper order. Say, "I'll put the black aces in the middle and the reds on the top and bottom." Actually, the reds go in the middle. After showing the first red ace and placing it (really the black ace) on the table, when you reverse count the three aces, one at a time, from the left hand to the right hand, you can call each card by its supposed color, i.e., "Black, black, red."

SPECIAL NOTE: In many cases, you can place the two "red" (really black) aces directly onto the spectator's outstretched palm. After you deal each card into the spectator's palm, have the spectator put the other hand flat on top of the cards. Apparently, this is so that you cannot do anything "tricky." In reality, this keeps the spectator from looking at the faces of the cards. With this form of presentation, the aces apparently change places while held tightly in the spectator's own hands!

SANDWICHED ACES

Here is a baffling four-ace routine that people will talk about and want to see again. Once you have mastered it, you will probably keep it as a highlight in your program. Best of all, only a few special moves are required, and they fit into the routine so neatly that there is little chance that anyone will begin to suspect them.

EFFECT

The magician openly deals the two black aces face down on the table. The spectator freely selects any card from the pack, say the five of diamonds. The five is turned face up and "sandwiched" between the two face-down black aces. The three cards are then turned over as a group and placed on top of the pack.

Without hesitation, the magician spreads the top two cards, showing that the five of diamonds has vanished from between the black aces. The magician deals the black aces onto the table and immediately spreads the pack face down along the table, revealing the two red aces face up in the center, with a single face-down card between them. "I knew your card was sandwiched between two aces," the magician declares. When a spectator turns over the face-down card, it proves to be the missing five of diamonds!

SECRET AND PREPARATION

The success of this trick depends on the proper setup of the four aces in the deck before the trick begins. From a regular pack of cards, remove the aces and arrange them in the following positions:

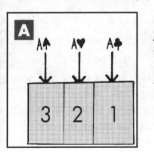

A Place the two black aces (ace of clubs and ace of spades) face down together and one of the red aces (ace of hearts in the illustrations) face down between them.

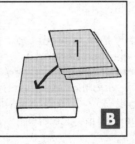

B Place this group of three cards on top of the face-down pack.

C Place the remaining red ace (ace of diamonds) face up on the bottom of the pack, and you're ready. (In the illustrations, the aces have been numbered 1 through 4 to make them easier to follow. 1 is the ace of clubs, 2 is the ace of hearts, 3 is the ace of spades, and 4 is the ace of diamonds. The selected card is indicated by an "X.")

METHOD

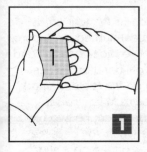

1 With the pack held in dealing position in the left hand, grasp the top card of the pack (1—the ace of clubs) between the thumb and fingers of your right hand in the same grip as if you were executing the DOUBLE LIFT.

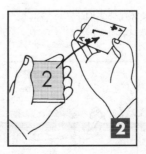

2 Do not do the DOUBLE LIFT! Just pick up the ace of clubs and turn it face up, showing it to the audience. Say, "The top card of the pack is the ace of clubs."

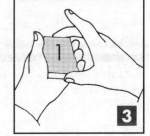

3 Replace the ace on top of the pack.

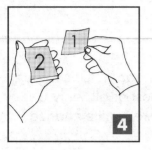

4 Without hesitation, take the ace of clubs with your right fingers and place it face down on the table. Say, "I will place it here on the table."

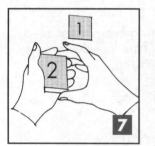

5 Secure a LITTLE FINGER BREAK between the next two cards on top of the pack (2—the ace of hearts and 3—the ace of spades).

6 Execute a DOUBLE LIFT, lifting both cards (as one) from the top of the pack. Turn them over, showing the face of what the spectators believe to be the top card (3—the ace of spades). As you display the ace, remark, "Here is the next card, the ace of spades..."

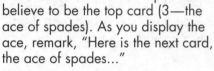

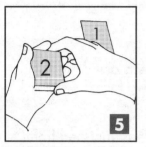

7 Replace the two cards back on the top of the pack.

8 Immediately take the real top card (2—the ace of hearts) from the top of the pack and place it face down next to the ace of clubs (1) on the table. Say, "...which I will place here, next to the ace of clubs."

NOTE: As it stands, you have one red ace and one black ace face down on the table. The spectators believe the two cards are the two black aces. The other black ace is really on top of the pack, and the last red ace is face up on the bottom of the deck.

9 Run through the pack face down and invite the spectator to select any card. When the card has been chosen, square the pack and hold it in dealing position in your left hand.

10 Instruct the spectator to turn the card face up and slide it between the two "black aces" on the table, thus sandwiching the card between them.

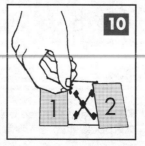

11 Secure a LITTLE FINGER BREAK under only the top card of the pack (3—the ace of spades). Because the attention of the audience is focused on what the spectator is doing, obtaining the LITTLE FINGER BREAK will go completely unnoticed.

12 Next, pick up the three cards on the table.

13 Place them on top of the pack, adding them to the ace of spades, and square all four cards together above the break.

14 Without hesitation, turn over all four cards (as three) face up on the pack, as shown.

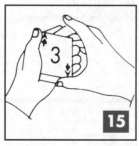

15 The two black aces will now be face up on top of the pack; the spectator's card will be face down below the aces, and below that will be the face-up ace of hearts.

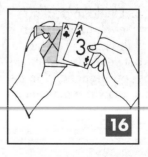

16 As soon as the four cards have been turned over, carefully take the two black aces (1 and 3) with your right hand and place them face up on the table. Remark, "Your card seems to have disappeared from between the two black aces." Be sure when you deal the two black aces off the pack that you do not shift the face-down card below them, accidentally exposing the face-up ace of hearts.

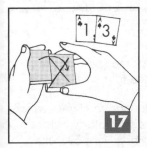

17 Holding the pack in your hands, give the deck a single cut. This places the face-up ace of diamonds, the bottom card, directly on top of the selected card and the face-up ace of hearts below it. You have automatically sandwiched the selected card between the two face-up red aces.

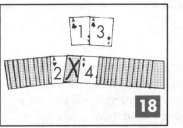

18 All that remains is to spread the pack face down on the table, revealing the two red aces and the face-down card between them. When the spectator turns over the sandwiched card, everyone will be amazed to see that the chosen card has mysteriously appeared between the two red aces, the ace of hearts and the ace of diamonds!

COMMENTS AND SUGGESTIONS

Precision, more than skill, is the main factor in this mystery, so practice can make it perfect. In showing the first black ace, display it just as if you were doing a DOUBLE LIFT, replacing it on the pack and dealing it face down as a single card. When you show and deal the ace of spades, your action is identical, so the DOUBLE LIFT will never be suspected.

DOUBLE THOUGHT PROJECTION

 This is an exceptionally fine mental effect, using only two ordinary packs of cards with contrasting backs, such as one red-backed deck and one blue-backed deck. It requires only one sleight, and you have already learned it!

EFFECT

The magician runs through a deck of cards face up and asks a spectator to freely name any card in the pack. Assume that the spectator selects the seven of diamonds. The performer removes this card from the pack and turns it face down, showing that it has a blue back. With that, the magician spreads the rest of the pack face down on the table, revealing that every card in the deck except the seven of diamonds has a red back! Then, to take the mystery one step further, the magician spreads the blue-backed deck face down on the table to reveal a single red-backed card right in the middle of the pack. When this card is turned face up, it is found to be the seven of diamonds from the red-backed deck!

SECRET AND PREPARATION

The only sleight used in this amazing mystery is the DOUBLE LIFT (see page 44).

You will need two matching decks of cards with different colored backs, say one red and one blue. Beforehand, remove a card from the blue-backed deck and place it on the bottom of the red-backed deck. (In the illustrations, this card is shown as the four of clubs; however, any card may be used.) Replace the red pack with the one blue card in its case and have the blue-backed pack lying openly on the table. In fact, you can use the blue pack for a few preliminary tricks if you wish, as the absence of a single card (the blue-backed four of clubs) will not be noticed.

METHOD

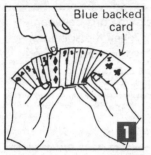

1 Bring out the case containing the red-backed pack and announce that you will mentally project the name of one card to the spectator. Fan or spread the cards face up in your hands and ask the spectator to name any card desired. Stress the fact that the spectator has absolutely free selection of any card.

Blue backed card

2 When the spectator names a card, in this case, the seven of diamonds, divide the pack into two sections at the place in the deck where the card is located. Keep the selected card at the top of the packet in your left hand.

NOTE: The four of clubs, the secret blue-backed card, is at the face of the right-hand packet.

3 As you comment about the fact that the spectator made a completely free selection, deal the seven of diamonds from the top of the left-hand packet directly on top of the blue-backed four of clubs in the right-hand packet.

4 Reassemble the halves of the pack, placing the right-hand packet on top of the left-hand packet. This leaves the spectator's card on the face of the deck with the blue-backed four just below it.

5 At this point, get ready for the DOUBLE LIFT by securing a LITTLE FINGER BREAK (see page 43) beneath the seven of diamonds and the blue-backed four of clubs under it.

6 As you remark that the spectator could have selected any card in the pack, execute the DOUBLE LIFT and turn the two cards over (as one), displaying the blue back of what the spectator believes to be the chosen card, the seven of diamonds. Actually,

the blue back the spectator sees belongs to the four of clubs.

7 To prove that you knew which card the spectator would choose all along, turn over the pack you are holding in your left hand and spread the deck face down on the table, showing them all to be red-backed cards. Be sure to keep the two cards in your right hand held firmly, as shown. (Remember, the audience thinks you are holding a single card.)

8 Immediately pick up the blue-backed pack (which has been sitting on the table all along) in your left hand and turn it face up.

9 Place the two cards (which the audience thinks is only one) face up on the face of the blue-backed pack as you remark that the blue-back seven of diamonds really belongs in the blue deck.

NOTE: What the spectator does not know is that the seven of diamonds you have just placed on the blue-backed deck is really a red-backed card, thanks to your secret four of clubs! You are now perfectly set up to add a double-barreled impact to this mystery.

10 Cut the deck, burying the seven of diamonds somewhere near the center.

11 The final proof of your miraculous powers comes when you spread the blue-backed deck face down to reveal one red-backed card in the center of the deck.

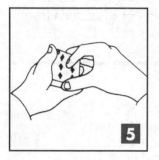

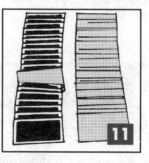

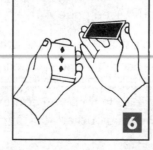

12 Remove the card and turn it face up to reveal it is the seven of diamonds, the only red-backed card in the blue deck.

CHAPTER 7
GLIDE TRICKS

When you add this sleight to your routine, you can practically duplicate the work of some of the greatest card experts. Once you have mastered THE GLIDE, you have taken a major step along the road to card magic. There are some excellent routines for it described in this section.

THE GLIDE

For directness, efficiency, and complete concealment, THE GLIDE rates high among card sleights. Simple though it is, it does require practice to be done properly and convincingly. THE GLIDE is an effective sleight, especially suited to beginners. It is equally valuable to all card workers, because it enables the magician to show a card and undetectably switch it for another.

EFFECT

You hold a pack of cards face up in your left hand. Call attention to the bottom card, say the two of clubs. Turning the pack face down, you draw out the bottom card with the tips of your right fingers and place it, still face down, on the table. When the card is turned over by a spectator, the two of clubs has changed into a totally different card!

METHOD

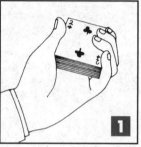

1 Hold the pack face up in your left hand with the thumb at one side and the fingers at the other side. The tips of the second, third, and little fingers should curl over the top of the pack and rest gently, as shown, against the face of the bottom card (the two of clubs).

NOTE: Your first finger remains on the side of the deck and does not touch the face of the bottom card.

2 Turn the left hand over, toward yourself, rotating your hand at the wrist.

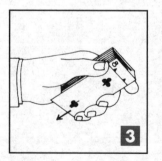

3 As soon as the pack is face down, with the tips of your left second, third, and little fingers, slide the bottom card back, so that it extends beyond the inner end of the pack about 1/2". From underneath, the deck now looks like this.

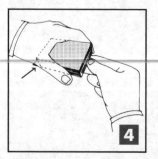

4 From above, the pack should appear to be completely natural, with the back of your hand hiding the protruding bottom card.

5 With your right hand, reach beneath the pack and press the tips of your right first and sec-

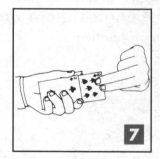

Bottom view

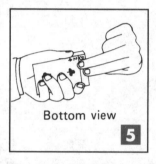

Audience view

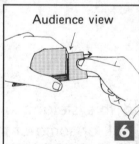

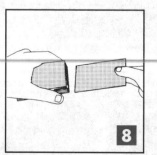

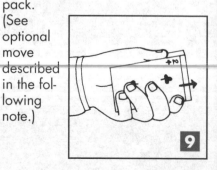

ond fingers against the face of the now exposed second card from the bottom (the eight of spades).

6 Begin to slide this card (the eight of spades) out from beneath the pack with the tips of your right fingers. When it is far enough out, place your right thumb on top of the card and draw it clear of the pack.

7 This is the view of the pack from the bottom.

8 Place the card on the table.

NOTE: The audience believes you have just pulled the bottom card (the two of clubs) from the deck. Really, you have removed the second card (the eight of spades).

9 As the right hand places its card on the table, use the left fingers to return the "glided" bottom card back to its original position, flush with the rest of the pack. (See optional move described in the following note.)

10 The card on the table can now be turned over to show that it has magically changed to a different card.

NOTE: If you find it difficult to return the glided card to its original position using only the second, third, and little fingers of the left hand, you may wish to use this optional move in Step 9. After the card has been removed by the right hand and is clear of the deck, extend your left first finger over the front of the deck. By a combination of pushing back with the left first finger and forward with the second, third, and little fingers, you will find that you can quite easily return the bottom card to its squared-up position on the bottom of the deck.

COMMENTS AND SUGGESTIONS

THE GLIDE may be performed with only a few cards, rather than the entire pack, and still be equally deceptive. As you practice, you will find that only a very light pressure from your left fingers is required to glide the bottom card back. Practice so that you can draw back only the bottom card, neatly and secretly, without having other cards tag along. Sometimes, you need a little more pressure, but always be careful not to apply too much. Also, many beginners, when learning THE GLIDE, hold the deck too tightly in the left hand. The pack should be held so that the back of the pack does not touch the palm of the left hand. Hold the deck so that just enough of your second, third, and little fingers extend around the bottom of the pack to touch the face of the card to be glided. When working with a new or borrowed pack, test THE GLIDE before using it, to get the "feel" of the cards. If necessary, the right fingers can actually take over the whole operation, by simply pushing back the bottom card and pulling out the next. However, this slows the action and should only be used in an emergency.

THE GLIDE
ALTERNATE METHOD

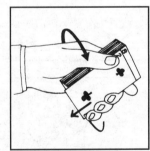

♠ After you have learned the basic glide, you may wish to add this extra touch. When you begin turning your hand over (Step 3 of THE GLIDE), begin at the same time to draw back the bottom card with the tips of your second and third fingers. If both the turning of the pack face down and THE GLIDE are executed simultaneously, the movement of your left fingers becomes even less detectable.

COLOR CHANGING ACES NO. 2
DOUBLE LIFT AND GLIDE

One good trick deserves another, and that rule applies to the second version of the COLOR CHANGING ACES. This method is very similar to the method already given (see page 47). However, this version depends on THE GLIDE (see page 54) as its second move instead of a second DOUBLE LIFT.

EFFECT

From the audience's view, the effect is identical to COLOR CHANGING ACES NO. 1 (see page 47). The magician displays the four aces. Holding them face down in a packet, the magician shows the face of both red aces while dealing them onto the table. Holding the two black aces, the magician commands the aces to change places. When the cards are turned over, the black aces are on the table, and the magician is holding the red aces!

METHOD

For this trick, you must do THE GLIDE (see page 54) and THE DOUBLE LIFT (see page 44).

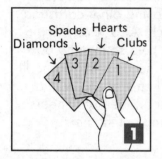

1 From a regular pack of cards, remove the four aces and place the rest of the deck aside. (In the illustrations, the aces have been numbered 1 through 4 to make them easier to follow.) As you display the aces, gather them into a packet and casually arrange them so that the aces alternate in color—starting with a black ace at the top of the face-down packet.

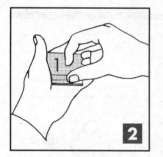

2 Place the packet face down in dealing position in the left hand.

3 Obtain a LITTLE FINGER BREAK (see page 43) beneath the top two cards of the packet (ace of clubs and ace of hearts).

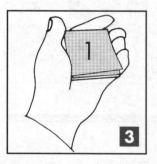

4 Using a DOUBLE LIFT, lift these two cards (as one) off the top of the packet and show the face of what the spectators believe to be the top card, the ace of hearts. At the same time, say, "Here is the ace of hearts, the top card of the pack."

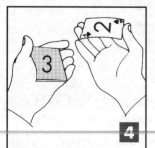

5 With that, replace the two cards on top of the packet.

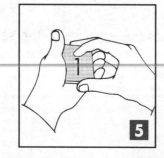

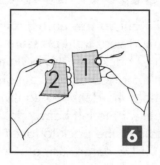

6 Deal the real top card, the ace of clubs, from the top of the packet to the table as you say, "I'll place the first red ace here on the table."

NOTE: So far, this follows exactly the COLOR CHANGING ACES NO. 1 routine, except for the color setup. Next comes the special added twist.

7 Instead of doing a reverse count and another DOUBLE LIFT, turn the packet face up in the left hand, in position to execute THE GLIDE. As you do this, point to the bottom card of the packet (the ace of diamonds) saying, "And here is the ace of diamonds, the other red ace."

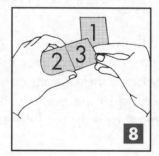

8 With that, turn the packet face down and execute THE GLIDE, drawing out the card second from the bottom (the ace of spades) instead of the real bottom card, the ace of diamonds.

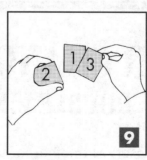

9 Place the card on the table as you say, "I'll put the ace of diamonds on the table along with the ace of hearts."

10 At this point, the trick is really over; all that's left is presentation. After a little byplay, turn over the two red aces in your hand to show that they have changed from black to red and invite a spectator to do the same with the black aces on the table!

COMMENTS AND SUGGESTIONS

As you arrange the aces in order (clubs, hearts, spades, and diamonds), you can miscall their position by remarking, "Blacks in the middle, reds on top and bottom." Then, using the DOUBLE LIFT, you apparently deal one red ace from the top. Immediately turning the packet face up, you supposedly deal the other red ace from the bottom.

One good presentation is to hold one pair face down in each hand and slap their free ends together, with an up and down action. Then, deliberately turn both pairs face up to show that they have magically changed places.

OIL AND WATER

"Dealing" tricks form a definite departure from other forms of card magic because they usually require only a small group of cards rather than a full pack. In addition, they generally get away from the usual procedure of having a spectator select a card from the pack. As a result, dealing tricks help to produce a varied program.

EFFECT

Six cards, three red and three black, numbering from ace through six, are arranged in alternating colors and number values. After displaying the cards in that manner, the magician turns them face down in the left hand and draws them, one at a time, from the bottom. The magician transfers them to the top, calling out their colors, "Red, black…" and so on. At intervals, individual cards are shown face up to prove that they are still in their alternating color order. The climax comes when the entire packet is turned face up and fanned. Amazingly, the cards have rearranged themselves into two separate groups. One is composed of three black cards; the other, of three red cards, all in perfect number order from ace to six!

SECRET AND PREPARATION

The only sleight used in this trick is THE GLIDE (see page 54).

From a regular pack of cards, remove the ace, deuce, and three of diamonds, and the four, five, six of spades. Arrange the six cards so they appear in the exact order shown. This accomplished, you are ready to begin.

METHOD

1 Fan the six cards face up and call attention to the fact that their number values are mixed and the cards alternate in color. Square up the packet of cards. Hold them face up in your left hand in position for THE GLIDE. Explain that, "like OIL AND WATER, red cards and black cards just don't mix."

NOTE: Make sure that the spectators understand that the cards in your hand alternate in color.

2 As you display the red ace at the face of the pack, call out "Red." Then, turn the left hand over so that the cards are face down. Remove the card from the bottom, the ace of diamonds, with your right fingers.

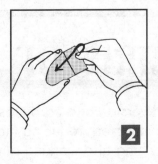

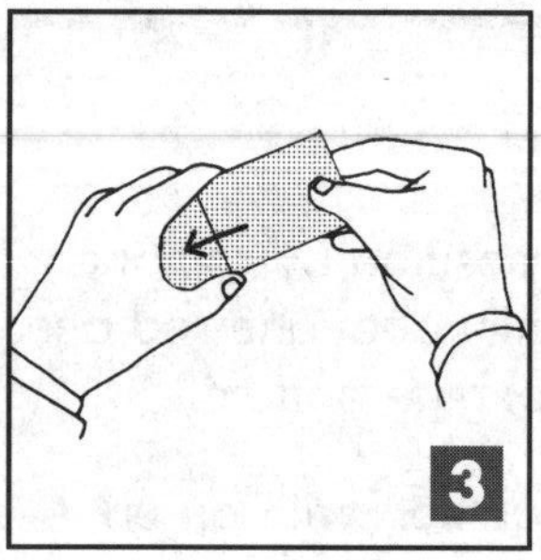

3 Place it on top of the packet. Do not do THE GLIDE, simply remove the ace from the bottom and move it to the top.

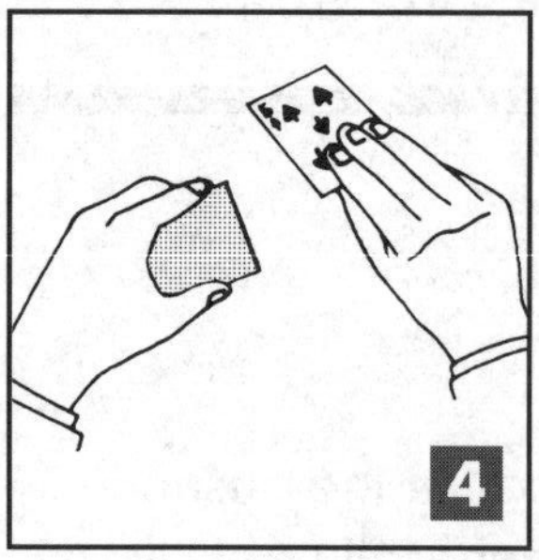

4 With the left hand still face down, remove the next card, the five of spades, from the bottom in your right fingers. To assure the audience that this card is, in fact, a black card, turn the five over to show its face. As you do this, say, "Black." Turn the card back over and place it face down on top of the packet.

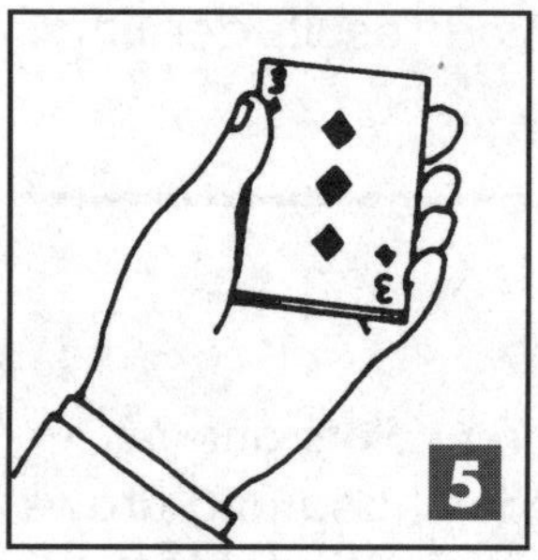

5 Again, turn the left hand over to show the face of the bottom card (the three of diamonds) to the spectators. Call out, "Red." Immediately, turn the packet face down, and this time, execute THE GLIDE, actually drawing out the card second from the bottom, the four of spades. Once the card has been removed from the bottom, place it face down on top of the pack of cards.

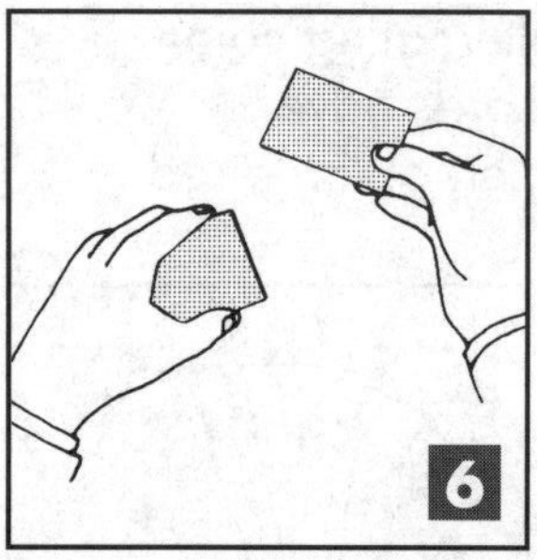

6 Still holding the cards face down in the left hand, draw out the bottom card of the pack, the three of diamonds, and hold it face down in your right hand. Pause for a moment as you call out, "Black." Do not turn this card face up. Instead, place the card face down on top of the packet.

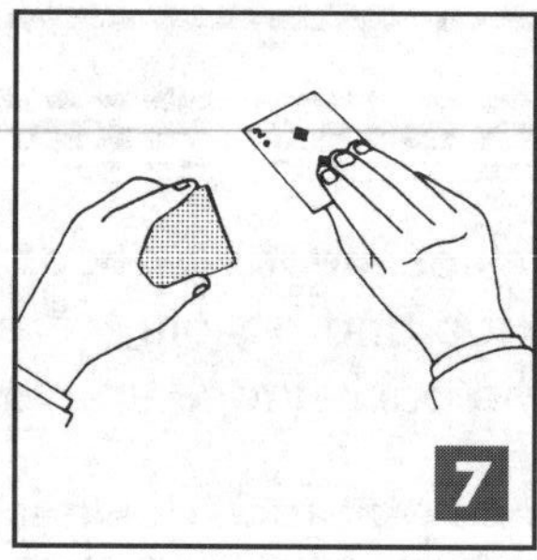

7 With the packet still face down, remove the bottom card of the pack, the two of diamonds, and turn it face up in the right hand. Pause for a moment, and call out, "Red." Then, place this card face down on top of the packet.

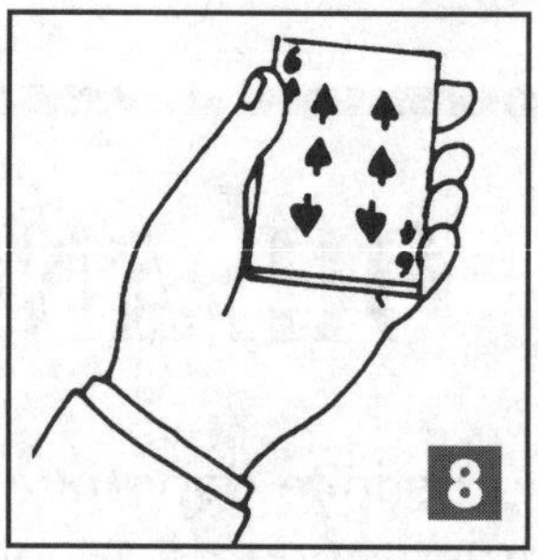

8 Finally, turn the packet face up, in position for THE GLIDE, and display the face of the six of spades as you say, "Black." Turn the pack face down and once again execute THE GLIDE, actually removing the second from the bottom card, the ace of diamonds. Place this card on top of the rest of the cards in the packet.

NOTE: Apparently, you have just shown each card in the packet, one at a time, without disturbing their alternate color or number order. Of course, you know that isn't the case!

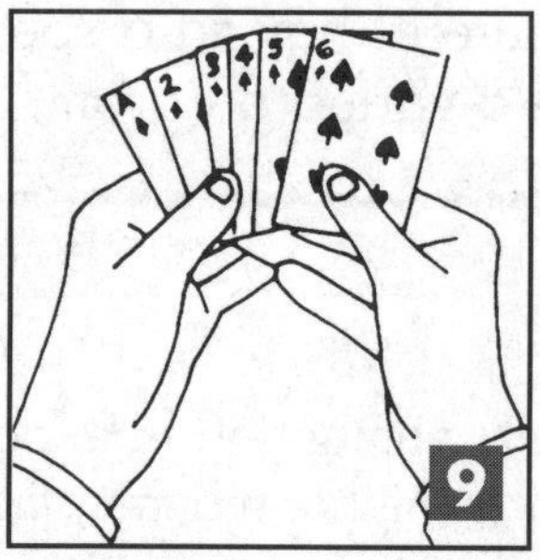

9 All that remains is to fan the packet face up, displaying that the cards have arranged themselves in numerical order, and that, like OIL AND WATER, red and black playing cards just don't mix.

COMMENTS AND SUGGESTIONS

Practice with the six cards until you memorize the routine, and this trick becomes virtually self-working. Its only move, THE GLIDE, should be done smoothly and at exactly the same pace as when you are really removing the bottom card. The total routine has been carefully designed so that each time you display a red card or black card, either on the bottom of the packet or in your right hand, you are psychologically convincing the spectators of the honesty of moving each card from the bottom to the top, diverting them from the real secret.

BIRDS OF A FEATHER

This is a modernized version of a card classic known as FOLLOW THE LEADER. Here, all difficult sleights have been eliminated, reducing the routine to a single, simple sleight, THE GLIDE (see page 54), with everything else working almost automatically.

EFFECT

From an ordinary pack, the magician removes five red cards, the ace through the five of diamonds, and five black cards, the ace through the five of clubs. Placing the ace of diamonds and the ace of clubs face up on the table to serve as "leaders," the magician deals the four remaining red cards face down on the red ace and the four remaining black cards face down on the black ace. The magician openly "transposes" the face-up aces, and at his command, the two deuces invisibly jump to the pile of the opposite color, each next to the ace of its own suit. Next, the face-down piles are transposed, and yet another pair of cards, this time the threes, follows in the same mysterious fashion, magically moving to their matching aces. This continues, transposing the piles in every possible combination. Yet, each time two cards are turned up, they prove to be a matching pair, having magically changed places to appear next to the aces of their own suits!

SECRET AND PREPARATION

From an ordinary pack, remove two groups of five cards—one group of red cards numbering ace through five, and one group of black cards with the same values. (In the illustrations, all clubs and diamonds have been used.) Place the two aces face up on the table and casually arrange the remaining eight cards in a fan from left to right in the following sequence: five of clubs, four of clubs, three of clubs, two of clubs, three of diamonds, four of diamonds, five of diamonds, and two of diamonds. (See illustration for Step 1.) With the cards arranged in this order, you are ready to begin.

METHOD

1 Display the eight cards in a face-up fan, pointing out that the cards are separated into two groups, red and black. Do not call attention to the numerical sequence of the cards. Shown casually, they will not appear to be in any special order.

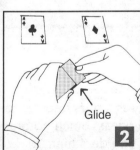

Glide

2 Close the fan and turn all the cards face down. Hold the packet in your left hand in position for THE GLIDE. Now, execute THE GLIDE, apparently dealing the bottom red card (really the second from the bottom) onto the table next to the ace of diamonds. Say, "I will deal the red cards here on the table next to their leader, the red ace of diamonds."

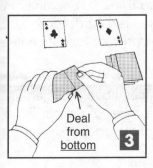

Deal from bottom

3 After dealing the second card from the bottom, do not return the bottom, glided card back to its former position. Instead, hold the card in its glided position and deal three more cards, one at a time, apparently from the bottom of the pack, onto the first card.

4 Stop dealing after you have the four cards face down in a pile next to the red ace. Because of THE GLIDE, the last card dealt on the red pile is really a black card.

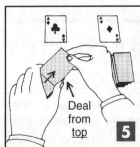

Deal from top

5 Square up the packet in your left hand (secretly bringing the glided card even with the rest of the packet) and deal the remaining cards, one at a time, from the top of the packet onto the table next to the black ace. As you deal these cards, say, "All the black cards go next to their leader, the black ace."

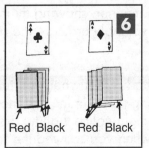

Red Black   Red Black

6 As shown in the illustration, unknown to the audience, you now have one red card on top of the black pile and one black card on top of the red pile. If you have executed THE GLIDE and the deal correctly, the rest of the trick will work automatically.

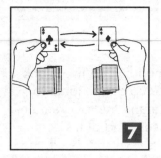

7 Exchange the positions of the two "leader" aces. Say, "No matter how I change the aces, the rest of the cards will 'Follow the Leader' and turn up in matching pairs."

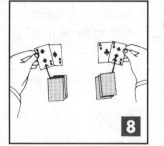

8 With that, turn over the top cards of both face-down packets. These two cards will be the deuces that match in suit and color their new, leader aces. Place the deuces face up on top of their correct color aces and continue.

9 Next, exchange the positions of the two face-down piles. Say, "Even if I switch the piles, it always works out the same."

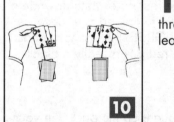

10 Turn over the top card of each pile, revealing the threes, as they, too, follow their leaders.

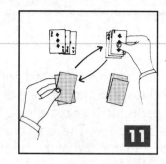

11 Exchange either pile of face-up cards with the face-down pile of cards diagonally across from it, as shown.

12 Turn over the top two cards from the face-down piles to show the matching fours. Place them on their respective leader packets.

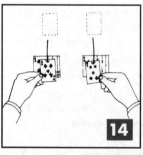

13 Exchange the other pile of face-up cards with the single face-down card diagonally across from it, as shown.

14 Turn over the remaining two face-down cards. These will be the fives that also match the color of their leader packets!

COMMENTS AND SUGGESTIONS

After practicing this trick until you can present it smoothly and without hesitation, you can add the following touch: Instead of starting with the cards in a prearranged sequence, begin by openly shuffling the four red cards and place them face down on the table. Shuffle the four black cards and place them face down on the red cards. Since no one knows the bottom card, you can glide it back and show the faces of the first three red cards, as you deal them to the table. The fourth card (really a black card) you deal on top of the red cards without showing it. Next, deal the first three black cards in the same manner, showing their faces and dealing the last card (really a red card) face down without showing it. Those two final cards are the first to follow the leader. The rest of the cards travel automatically as already described.

The one disadvantage to this method is that when you turn over each set of cards to show that they have changed piles, the cards will not be matching pairs. In the first method, however, if you were to show the faces of the cards before you dealt them, someone might notice that the first red card you deal from "the bottom of the packet" is not the card they saw on the bottom when you showed the fan at the start.

CHAPTER 8

SHORT CARD TRICKS

The short card is one of the most useful devices ever designed for card magic. It can be used for locating, forcing, or even vanishing a card. It will pass totally unsuspected by even the keenest observers. As its name implies, it is a card that is "shorter" than those in the rest of the pack and can be simply and easily prepared with any deck.

HOW TO MAKE A SHORT CARD

1 To make a short card, first draw a ruled line 1/32" from both ends of a standard playing card.

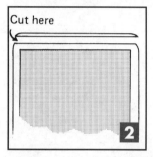

1/32 of an inch

2 With a pair of sharp scissors, carefully trim off the ends using the ruled line as a guide.

3 Next, "round" all four of the cut corners so they will match the corner of the regular cards in the pack.

Cut here

NOTE: For rounding corners, a pair of curved manicure scissors is helpful, but ordinary scissors will also work. Just cut the corners very carefully.

Short Card

4 This illustration compares a short card with a regular card from the same pack. As you can see, it would be difficult for anyone to detect the short card when it is mixed with the regular cards in the pack.

5 Some magicians carry a pair of small "fold-away" scissors with them, to use with a borrowed deck. All you have to do is to secretly pocket a card from the borrowed deck. Then, work some trick, such as a "mental" effect, in which you leave the room. While outside, you cut the end from the card and round the corners. You can then return the card to the pack later. The pack can still by used by its owner in regular card games, without the players ever realizing that one of the cards has been shortened.

COMMENTS AND SUGGESTIONS

For purposes of practice, you can make your first short card from the joker (or the extra joker, if the pack has one). In this way, you can then either add the joker when you wish to do a short card trick, or you can later shorten any other regular card after you have learned how to use your practice short card.

HOW TO RIFFLE
THE SHORT CARD TO THE TOP

No matter where the short card may be in the pack, you can find it almost instantly by sense of touch alone in a number of ways. (In all of the following illustrations, the short card is indicated by an "S.")

METHOD

1 Squeeze the shuffled pack and hold it in dealing position in your left hand. Cut the pack a few times by riffling the inner end of the deck with your right thumb.

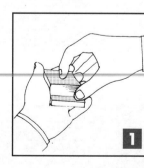

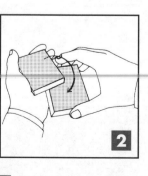

2 Stop your riffle about halfway through the pack and transfer the remaining upper half to the bottom of the pack to complete the cut.

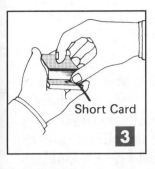

3 On your last cut, when you riffle the inner end of the pack upward with your thumb, if you listen and feel with your thumb, you will notice a slight "snap" when you reach the short card. When this happens, stop your riffle. Make your cut, lifting off all of the cards above the short card.

Short Card

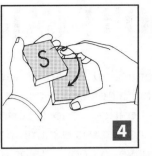

4 Complete the cut by placing this upper packet beneath the lower, as shown. This puts the short card on top of the pack.

SHORT CARD TO BOTTOM

♥ In some tricks, it may be necessary to control the short card to the bottom of the pack instead of the top. This can be done in several ways.

FIRST METHOD

Bring the short card to the top of the pack as just described in HOW TO RIFFLE THE SHORT CARD TO TOP (see page 62). Then, using the OVERHAND SHUFFLE CONTROL – TOP CARD TO BOTTOM (see page 33), shuffle the top card (the short card) to the bottom of the deck. You have not only placed the short card where you want it, on the bottom of the pack, at the same time you have convinced the spectators that all the cards in the pack are well mixed.

SECOND METHOD

A second method of bringing the short card to the bottom of the pack is simplicity itself. After your riffle which places the short card on top, simply turn the pack face up in your left hand. Proceed with the instructions for SHORT CARD TO TOP, as described. This brings the short card to the top of the face-up pack; if you turn the pack over, the short card will be at the bottom!

THIRD METHOD

Of the three methods described, this is the cleanest and quickest method of getting the short card to the bottom of the deck, although it will require a bit more practice. In the first method, you have to riffle the card to the top and then shuffle it to the bottom. In the second method, the deck must be held face up and the short card may be noticed, particularly if you are doing a number of tricks in which the same short card is used. This third method avoids both of the "shortcomings" (pardon the pun) of the previous two methods.

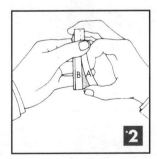

1 Hold the deck in your left hand as if you were starting to perform an overhand shuffle. Your right hand grasps the deck with the first finger on the face of the pack, your other three fingers cover the outside end, and your thumb is at the end nearest you, as shown.

2 Riffle the deck downward with your right thumb, starting with the top card. When you get to the short card and hear and/or feel the "snap," stop your riffle.

3 Either cut the bottom portion to the top of the pack or overhand shuffle the bottom portion to the top of the pack, leaving the short card on the bottom.

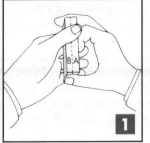

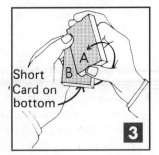

Short Card on bottom

SHORT CARD AS LOCATOR

Once you have controlled the short card to the top of the pack, you can use it effectively as a "locator" for finding other cards as well. This is highly baffling to those spectators who think they have followed a trick up to a certain point, only to find that it goes completely beyond their idea of how it's done. This is a combination, consisting of the short card and the Hindu shuffle, that is always effective, as each helps the other to gain results that neither could gain alone.

EFFECT

A card is freely chosen from the pack. The spectator is allowed to replace it wherever desired. The magician gives the pack a thorough, genuine shuffle. Then the magician causes the card to appear on top of the pack or finds it in some other unaccountable way. In brief, this method can be used as a very baffling card control in many standard tricks.

METHOD

1 A short card is already in the pack and is brought to the bottom by the RIFFLE – SHORT CARD TO TOP (see page 62) method. From then on, the trick is handled in conjunction with the Hindu shuffle and standard RIFFLE SHUFFLE (see page 8).

2 With the short card on the bottom of the pack, spread the cards and let a spectator take any one desired. Tell the spectator to show the card to the audience before returning it to the pack.

3 This gives you ample time to square the pack in readiness for the Hindu shuffle. Don't actually begin shuffling until the spectator is about ready to return the card to the pack; otherwise, you may have to go through the shuffle more than once, and this is apt to slow the action.

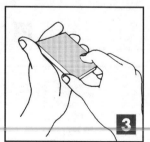

4 Proceed with the regular Hindu shuffle, drawing back the lower portion of the pack with your right hand. Keep the short card on the bottom of the packet in your right hand as you draw off small batches of cards with the fingers of your left hand. Tell the spectator to say, "Stop," at any time during the shuffle.

Short Card **4**

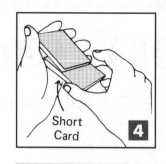

Short Card **5**

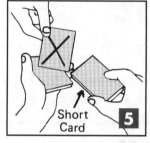

6

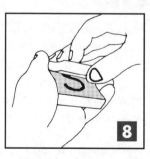

S **8**

S **9**

5 Let the spectator return the chosen card (X) on the portion of the pack resting in your left hand. Drop the right-hand packet on the left hand cards, as with the HINDU KEY-CARD LOCATION (see page 21). In this case, the short card becomes the key card, as it is placed directly on the selected card (X).

6 Square the pack, cut it, and give it a regular riffle shuffle, riffling the ends of the two halves of the pack together. This can be repeated, and it will not separate the two cards, because the short card (S) will ride along with the longer selected card (X). (Try this shuffle a few times to see how well it works.)

7 Tap the end of the pack on the table to make sure that the short card is down in the pack.

8 Continue shuffling, and after each shuffle, square and tap the pack. Finally, riffle the inner end upward with your right thumb. You will note the click when you come to the short card. Cut the pack at that point. The short card (S) will stay on top of the lower packet.

9 In cutting, place the right-hand packet beneath the left-hand packet. This will automatically bring the short card (S) to the top, with the selected card (X) just beneath it. Thus, you have used your key card to bring a chosen card to the top without looking through the pack; and you have legitimately shuffled the pack as well!

10 Since you now know the position of the selected card in the pack, you may proceed with any "discovery" that you wish.

COMMENTS AND SUGGESTIONS

The SHORT CARD AS LOCATOR can be used in any trick where you must first bring a chosen card to the top of the pack. In Step 10, the selected card (X) is actually second from the top, but you can handle that quite easily. One way is to turn up the top card, asking if it was the card the spectator took. The answer, of course, will be, "No." Push the short card face down into the middle of the pack, saying that you will find the card in a most mysterious way, which you are now prepared to do.

SURPRISE DISCOVERY
SHORT CARD AS LOCATOR

METHOD

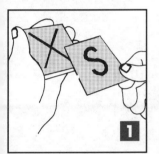

1 For an immediate and effective discovery of the chosen card, you can proceed as follows: Take the short card (S) from the pack, removing it face down with your right hand. Tap the short card on top of the pack and tell the spectator that this will cause the selected card to rise to the top of the pack.

2 Since the selected card (X) is already there, the trick is really done. For added effect, you should thumb the top card (X) onto the table, then casually replace the short card (S) on top of the pack, as though it had played no real part in the trick.

3 Have the spectator turn up the card on the table (X). To everyone's surprise, it will be the very card the spectator selected! If you prefer, you can have the spectator name the card and let someone else turn it up. This will dumbfound the spectators, particularly those who did not see the spectator's card when it was removed from the pack by the spectator.

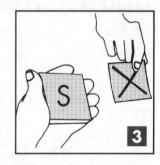

QUICK RIFFLE LOCATION

◆ This form of the SHORT CARD AS LOCATOR (see page 64) is very effective when done briskly and convincingly. It forms a nice variation from the usual "location."

METHOD

Have the short card either on the bottom or on the top to start. While the spectator is looking at the chosen card, cut the short card to the center of the pack. Then, riffle the pack for the card's return, but stop at the short card. The spectator's card is replaced in the pack where you stopped, on top of the short card. You can then locate the card by riffling the short card to the top of the pack. This automatically brings the spectator's card to the bottom where you can reveal it in any manner you wish.

CHAPTER 9
GIANT CARD TRICKS

Giant cards, available in most toy and novelty stores, represent a comparatively new type of magic that has grown in popularity. Since the cards are four times as large as ordinary playing cards, they have little in common where manipulation is concerned. Their added thickness makes the giants more cumbersome to handle. However, they can be dealt face down or face up and shown in a fan in the same way as smaller cards, which makes them adaptable to certain tricks.

Giant cards can also be identified by suit and value, so that the discovery of chosen cards in giant sizes can be worked in conjunction with cards from ordinary packs. Such tricks will be found in this section along with a variety of other effects.

Most important is the use of giant cards when performing for large audiences, where smaller card effects would be less effective and those of the "table" type would be lost entirely. "The bigger the audience, the bigger the cards" is the rule in this case, just as with any other magical appliances.

When working before smaller audiences, you can reserve a giant card trick for a "smash" ending to a regular card routine. People are always impressed by a climax that tells them that the show is over, and a giant-card finish will fill that purpose perfectly.

BIGGER CARD TRICK

 A bit of comedy usually adds spice to a mystery, and this trick stands as a good example. By having it ready, you can inject it at a timely moment, depending on the mood of your audience. It can also serve as a prelude to a more ambitious effect.

EFFECT

A card is selected and returned to the pack. The magician shuffles and places the pack in a paper bag. Showing that the right hand is empty, the magician thrusts it into the bag, announcing that the chosen card will be found with a "magic touch." The magician brings out a card, such as the three of clubs, and shows it triumphantly, only to have the spectator who selected the card say it is the wrong card. The magician asks the spectator if the card was a "bigger card." The spectator replies, "Yes." The magician tries and fails again. The card is still not big enough. This third time, the magician is successful and brings out the chosen card, the nine of hearts, which is not only bigger in value, but proves to be four times bigger in size, for it emerges in the form of a giant card!

SECRET AND PREPARATION

A All that is required for this effect is a regular pack of cards, an ordinary paper bag, and one giant card. The giant card should be a seven or higher in value.

B Place the giant card (in the illustration, the nine of hearts) inside the paper bag.

C Fold the bag flat and place it aside. Find the nine of hearts in the regular pack and place it in position in the pack, ready for one of the card forces you have learned.

METHOD

1 Begin by forcing the nine of hearts by any method you have learned. After the audience has seen the card, have it returned to the pack and have the pack thoroughly shuffled by a spectator. When the deck is returned to you, thumb through the deck and say something like, "Well, you have mixed so thoroughly that I certainly couldn't find your card just by looking. So, I'll find it without looking at all!" As you run through the deck, pick any two "smaller" value cards and place them on top of the deck.

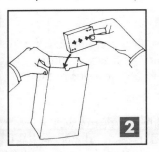

2 Pick up the folded bag and shake it open. Be careful to keep the giant card inside the bag as you do this. Place the deck into the bag. Do not disturb the cards as you put them in so that you will be able to find the two small cards on top of the deck.

3 Once the cards are in the bag, announce that you will attempt to find the selected card by your magic touch alone. With that, reach into the bag and pretend to grope

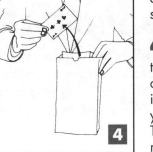

around, as if searching for the spectator's card.

4 Actually, grasp the top card of the deck (the three of clubs in the illustration). After a few seconds, remove the three and show it to the audience triumphantly, as you remark, "Here is your card!" The answer will be that it is not the right card. Act puzzled for a moment and then ask, "Was yours a bigger card?" Naturally, the spectator will reply, "Yes."

5 Place the three aside and repeat the procedure, removing the second small card from the top of the pack.

6 Now, even more puzzled, reach into the bag as you say, "Even bigger?" Remove the giant nine of hearts and ask, "Well, is this big enough?" The audience will not only be surprised that you have found the correct card, they will be amazed that it has grown to four times its normal size!

COMMENTS AND SUGGESTIONS

Handle the paper bag casually, as though it had nothing really important to do with the trick. If you present the effect in a serious vein, as if you were honestly attempting to find the spectator's card through your sense of touch, it will turn the climax into a real comedy surprise when you produce the much bigger card.

SYMPATHETIC CARDS

♦ Here is a really magical effect performed with any standard pack of cards and a giant card. No special skill is required; proper timing is the important factor. Therefore, the trick should be carefully rehearsed until you are familiar with the entire procedure. After that, the presentation will become almost automatic. You may be amazed by the way it will mystify your audiences, even at the closest range, because the trick depends on a subtle principle that truly deceives the eye.

EFFECT

The magician displays an ordinary deck and asks a spectator to shuffle it until the cards are well mixed. Holding the pack face down in one hand and a giant card face down in the other hand, the magician begins dealing cards, one at a time, onto the back of the giant card. The performer tosses the cards, again, one at a time, into a pile on the table.

This continues, card by card, as the magician tells the spectator to give the order to "Stop!" at any card desired. When the spectator does this, the magician remarks what a magical coincidence it would be if both the giant card and the card from the pack which the spectator selected were identical. The magician then turns both cards face up, revealing them to be exactly the same!

SECRET AND PREPARATION

The only items you need for this effect are a giant card and an ordinary pack of cards from which the duplicate of the giant card is removed in advance. To prepare, place the giant card face down on top of the regular-size duplicate card. Hold both cards in your right hand, with your fingers beneath, keeping the duplicate small card and your thumb on top of the giant card. (In the illustrations, the giant card and its duplicate are the ace of hearts. The duplicate, regular-size ace of hearts is indicated with an "X.")

METHOD

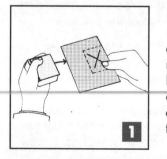

1 Hand the pack to a spectator to shuffle. Pick up the giant card and (secretly) the duplicate regular card in your right hand. Hold the two cards face down above the table, as shown. Be careful not to show the face(s) of the card(s).

NOTE: For a clever method of pre-setting the giant card and its duplicate which makes the "pickup" of the two cards quite easy, please see Comments and Suggestions at the end of this trick.

2 After the spectator is satisfied that the cards are well mixed, and you have the giant card and its secret duplicate held firmly in your right hand, pick up the shuffled deck in your left hand. Hold the pack in dealing position, as shown in Step 1.

NOTE: You may find it easier to position the shuffled pack in your left hand first, and then pick up the giant card and its duplicate. In that case, just reverse Steps 1 and 2.

3 Tell the audience that you are not going to show the face of the giant card. Explain that you are doing this for a special reason, since the object of the mystery is for the spectator to magically determine the suit and value of the giant card without knowing it.

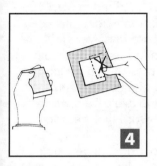

4 Deal the top card from the pack in your left hand, face down, onto the back of the giant card, as shown. (Just push the card from the top of the pack onto the back of the giant card with your left thumb.)

5 Pause a moment and then tilt the giant card, allowing the smaller card to slide off the giant card and drop, face down, on the table.

6 With your left hand, deal the next (top) card from the pack onto the back of the giant card in exactly the same way. After a brief pause, your right hand tilts the giant card, letting the smaller card slide off, landing on top of the first card already on the table. Continue thumbing off cards, one by one, onto the back of the giant card, then letting them slide onto the pile of cards on the table.

7 Ask the spectator to say, "Stop!" at any time as you deal through the deck.

NOTE: Be careful that none of the regular cards turns face up as you slide them from the giant card onto the pile of cards on the table.

8 Stop when the call comes. If you are in the middle of a deal, or if you are sliding one of the regular cards onto the pile on the table, ask the spectator which card is being selected. This proves that you are giving the spectator every opportunity to make a free choice. Whatever the final decision, see that the selected card is positioned on the back of the giant card as shown in Step 6.

NOTE: Here is the situation at this point: The giant card is held in your right hand. It acts as a tray for the spectator's freely selected card which rests on the back of the giant card. Unknown to the audience, with your right fingers, you are holding the secret duplicate of the giant card underneath the giant card.

9 Spread the remainder of the cards that you are holding in your left hand face up on the table with your left hand. As you spread the left-hand packet face up, remind the audience that the spectator could have chosen any of those cards.

10 Pick up the pile of cards already dealt, and turn them all face up. Casually spread them on the table, as shown. State, "If the spectator had stopped me sooner, one of these would have been chosen."

11 As you make the statement about the already dealt cards in Step 10, your left hand moves its fingers beneath the giant card. With your left fingers, hold the regular duplicate card against the bottom of the giant card. Your left thumb holds the spectator's selected card above. This allows your right hand to release its grip on the giant card and the secret duplicate card.

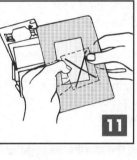

12 With the first finger of your right hand, point to the selected card lying on top of the giant card. Say, "Out of all the different cards in the pack, this is the card you chose."

NOTE: In transferring the giant card from your right hand to your left hand, you have subtly convinced the audience that all is fair, as both hands are obviously quite empty.

13 The following three steps (13, 14, and 15) are the most important in the routine. Study them carefully. Your right hand now returns to its former position so that the fingers of your right hand also hold the duplicate card under the giant card. Your left fingers release their hold on the duplicate card, but your left thumb continues to press against the spectator's selected card on top of the giant card, as shown in Step 11.

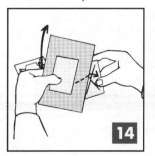

14 You begin three actions that take place simultaneously. First, both hands begin tilting the audience end of the giant card upward. Second, at the same time, your right fingers begin to draw the secret duplicate card to the right, off the face of the giant card. Third, with your left thumb, retain the spectator's selected card on top of the giant card.

15 Continue rotating the giant card so that the face of the giant card is toward the audience. You secretly retain the spectator's selected card on top of the giant card with your left thumb. With your right fingers, draw the hidden duplicate card, face up, fully into view. You have now undetectably switched the selected card for the secret duplicate card. To the spectator, it will appear that you are merely turning the selected card and the giant card face up at the same time. This is a totally convincing move.

NOTE: At this point, the spectator's card is hidden under the face-up giant card. The duplicate regular card, which matches the giant card, is face up in your right hand. To your audience, it will appear as though the duplicate card came off the back of the giant card, instead of from below.

16 Casually place the giant card face up on the face-up pile of cards on the table. The hidden selected card falls unnoticed beneath the giant card and becomes another of the miscellaneous face-up cards in the pile of cards on the table.

17 Drop the duplicate regular card face up on the giant card, proving that the spectator has miraculously picked the exact duplicate of the giant card from the pack!

18 The trick is now over. However, at this point, you can add a subtle touch by picking up the giant card and its duplicate from the table and handing them to the spectator. As you hand them over, turn both cards over, showing the backs to

be unprepared. The original selected card lies forgotten in the mass of cards on the table.

IMPORTANT NOTE: This entire, very clever effect hinges on the secret move (Steps 13, 14, 15). This is when you secretly switch the spectator's selected card for the duplicate card under the giant card. Here is the sequence as seen by the spectators.

19 As described in Step 13, your right hand moves to the giant card and your right fingers grasp the secret duplicate card and press it against the bottom of the giant card. Then, both hands start to rotate the giant card, face up, toward the spectator.

20 Your right fingers begin to slide the duplicate card off the face of the giant card. Your left thumb maintains its pressure on the selected card on top of the giant card.

21 The selected card is now hidden by the giant card, as your right hand continues sliding the duplicate card to your right.

22 Your left hand drops the giant card and the selected card face up on the pile of face-up cards already on the table. Your right hand displays the duplicate small card as if it were the freely selected card.

COMMENTS AND SUGGESTIONS

If you wish to perform this effect during your card routine, rather than at the start, you can use the following setup:

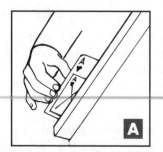

A Place the giant card and its regular duplicate on the edge of the table so that they both overlap the edge. You may then present any card effects which do not involve the duplicate card.

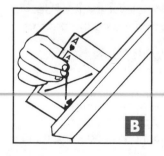

B When you are ready to perform the SYMPATHETIC CARDS, reach over with your right hand and pick up the giant card and the secret duplicate card, as shown. You are now all set to present this extremely clever close-up mystery.

If more convenient, you may also place the giant card and the secret duplicate card on a book, ashtray, or some other handy object that is already on the table, rather than placing the two cards on the edge of the table. Just be sure that both the giant card and the secret duplicate can be easily picked up at the same time.

NOTE: In the switch of the duplicate for the spectator's card, timing is the key factor. For best results, you should practice

in front of a mirror. The draw-off should begin as the edge of the giant card is level with the eyes of the spectators. That is the time when the ends of all three cards are toward the spectators. At that instant, the spectators lose sight of the backs before they see the faces. When your right hand draws the card to the right, as it comes into view, look at it. The audience will follow your eyes, never suspecting that the card they are watching came from the front and not the back of the giant card. This is another excellent example of misdirection.

APPLAUSE CARD

The APPLAUSE CARD provides a surprise ending for a card routine in which a clever trick is followed by a comedy gag. Audiences appreciate such touches and, even if you have patterned your program along serious lines, it is often good to conclude your show with a magical comedy closing effect such as this one.

EFFECT

A spectator selects a card and returns it to the pack, which is then thoroughly shuffled. The audience is told that the magician will produce the chosen card by using the sense of touch alone. The magician places the pack in an inside coat pocket. After several wrong cards are removed, the magician reaches into the pocket and brings out the spectator's card, but it is now a giant-size card! When the audience applauds, a banner that says, "Thank you," drops from beneath the giant card.

SECRET AND PREPARATION

A The props needed for this effect are a deck of cards, a jumbo or giant card, and a piece of light colored paper approximately 2' long and 3" wide. With a heavy marking pen, print the words, "Thank You," or some other appropriate phrase such as "Good-bye" or "Applause" down the length of the paper, allowing enough blank space (about half the length of the large card) at the top of piece of paper before beginning the lettering. Then, pleat the strip of paper, accordion fashion, as shown.

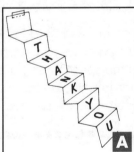

B Attach the top of the banner to the center of the back of a giant card (in this case, the four of diamonds) with a piece of tape, as shown. Also, tape a quarter to the unlettered side of the banner near the very bottom. The quarter will act as a weight and cause the banner to open quickly.

C Fold the banner and hold it against the back of the giant card. Place the giant card in your inside coat pocket with the face side of the card toward the audience.

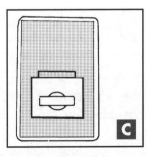

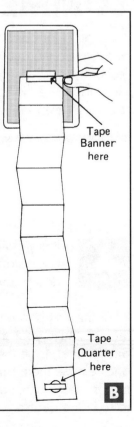

METHOD

1 From a regular-size pack of cards, force the four of diamonds on the spectator using any of the forcing methods previously explained (see pages 22, 38, and 41). After the card is noted by the spectator and shown to the rest of the audience (but, of course, not to you), let the spectator replace the card anywhere in the deck and have any member of the audience thoroughly shuffle the pack.

2 Be sure that the spectator is satisfied that the card is lost in the shuffled deck and that you could not possibly know where it is. If the spectator wishes, the deck may be shuffled again. When the spectator is completely satisfied, state that your super sensitive fingers will now find the card, while the deck is hidden from view in your pocket. Place the deck in the same inside coat pocket that contains the giant card.

NOTE: When you take the shuffled deck back from the spectator, casually look at the first two cards on the face of the deck to make sure that neither is the four of diamonds. If either one of them is the four, just remove the cards from the bottom of the deck, instead of from the top of the deck, in Step 3.

3 Reach into your pocket and remove one of the regular cards that you know is not the four of diamonds. Display the card triumphantly and ask the spectator if you are correct. The spectator will reply, "No." Say that this is an extremely difficult trick, and you will try again. Remove the second card, and, with a bit less confidence, ask the spectator if this is the one. Again, the response is, "No."

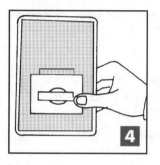

4 You become even more embarrassed. You might say something like, "I hope none of you has any place you were planning to be soon, as we have fifty cards left to go." Then, ask the spectator to help by concentrating on the card. Say, "Just make a big mental picture of it." Reach into your coat pocket and get ready to remove the giant card. Be sure to hold the pleated banner with your thumb so that it does not unfold.

5 Ask the spectator to name the card, and at the same time, remove the giant card.

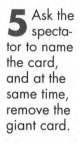

6 As you show the huge four of diamonds, and the spectator acknowledges that you have at last found the right card, say something like, "Well, I see you really did make a big mental picture!"

7 The unexpected appearance of the giant card will always get a laugh and applause. As the spectators react to this first surprise, draw back your right thumb and allow the banner to unfold to reveal your "Thank You" message. This is sure to get an even greater response from your audience.

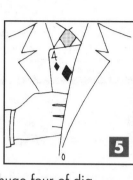

COMMENTS AND SUGGESTIONS

This particular card trick can be seen by a large group of a hundred or more people, particularly if you leave the stage and go into the audience to have the card selected. While your back is turned, have the spectator show the card to the rest of the audience. Have the spectator replace the card in the deck and return to the stage. If more convenient, you may also have the spectator join you on the stage for the selection of the card and the follow-up comedy discovery. This is a very clever comedy effect as well as good magic. It makes an excellent closing number for your show.

DOUBLE APPLAUSE CARD

It is possible to tape two or more pleated banners on the same giant card for a repeated comedy effect. For instance, the first banner can say "Thank You," and the second can read, "Both of You." For a birthday party, try "Thank You" and then "Happy Birthday, Mary," etc.

After the first banner falls, simply tear it off and set it aside, still keeping the second banner in place with your thumb. Move your thumb, allowing the second banner to fall for the double-barreled impact. When using more than one banner, tape them directly above one another so you are able to hold them both in position with your thumb and release them one at a time. You can also print the second message on the back of the banner. In this case, just turn the card around after the audience reads the front side of the banner. You'll need to make the banner "double" to hide the quarter you are using as a weight.

CHAPTER 10

SPECIAL
CARD TRICKS

Certain card tricks can be classified as "special" because they depend on methods or procedures that are somewhat unusual. Since they belong in no other category, they deserve one of their own; the term, "special," most adequately defines it.

In a sense, these are advanced card tricks; not necessarily because they are difficult to perform, but because they are the type that a performer is apt to add to a program after having mastered tricks of a more general nature. Test these "specials" by incorporating them into your regular program, one by one, and see for yourself how effective they are in enhancing the overall variety of your card mysteries.

SELF-REVERSING PACK

EFFECT

The magician shows an ordinary pack and begins to demonstrate various ways used to shuffle cards. Finally, taking the pack in both hands, the magician gives it a peculiar shuffle by repeatedly mixing batches of face-up cards with face-down cards, until the whole pack is a hopeless jumble. Then, giving the pack a single tap, the magician spreads the cards on the table and shows that the entire pack has regained its normal order with every card in the deck in its original face-down position.

METHOD

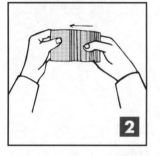

1 Begin by demonstrating various shuffles used with a pack of cards, such as the overhand shuffle, the Hindu shuffle, the riffle shuffle, etc.

2 Square the pack and hold it face down in your right hand with your thumb on top. Slide a small batch of cards from the top of the deck into your left fingers, gripping them as shown.

3 Turn your left hand over, so that its cards are face up. Then, your right hand slides another batch of face-down cards from the top of the pack beneath the face-up cards in the left hand.

4 The left hand turns over again, retaining its grip on both of the packets that have been moved off. The right thumb pushes more cards from the top of the deck to the left, so that the left hand (now thumb upward) can use its fingers to take these along beneath its group.

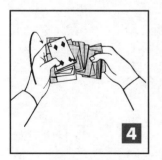

5 This process of sliding batches of cards from the top of the pack to the left, beneath the cards held in the left hand, continues as the left hand alternately turns over to receive some face up and some face down. This is repeated until all the cards in the right hand have been transferred to the left.

NOTE: Actually, instead of mixing the pack, you are dividing it into two sections, back to back. The face-up cards are never really intermingled with the face-down cards, although to the spectators, that appears to be the case.

6 Square the pack, remarking something like, "The cards are now hopelessly mixed, with batches of face-down cards among the face-up cards." To further demonstrate the mixed-up nature of the deck, cut deep in the pack and turn your right hand palm upward stating, "Here you see some cards back to face," as you show the face of the card on the right-hand packet and the back of the card on the left-hand packet.

7 Reassemble the two halves and cut the pack again, but this time, cut near the top of the pack. Turn the right hand palm upward adding, "And here are cards that happen to be face to back." Show as in Step 6, but since you now are in the top half of the pack, the right-hand packet will show a back, while the left packet will show a face.

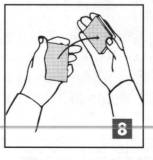

8 Reassemble the deck again and cut it once more. This time, cut at the spot where the two groups meet back to back. You will find this easy to do. Because of the natural bend in a deck of cards, when a portion of the deck is reversed on itself, there is a definite break between the two sections, making it very simple to find. When you locate the spot where the halves meet, separate the two sections and turn the right hand palm upward, saying, "And here are some others that are back to back."

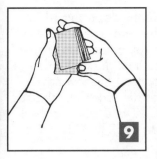

9 Instead of turning the right hand palm downward to replace the packet the way it was, reassemble the pack, leaving the right-hand packet palm upward. Just slide the right-hand packet on top of the left-hand packet. This maneuver turns the upper half (the face-up cards) face down on the rest of the face-down pack. All of the cards are now face down.

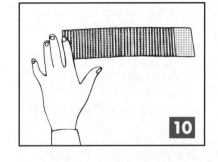

10 Holding the pack in your left hand, say, "Now for some real magic. One little tap," and you tap the pack with your right forefinger, "and all those mixed-up cards turn face down, as they were originally." Spread the pack face down on the table to show all backs. Your magic tap worked!

COMMENTS AND SUGGESTIONS

No real skill is required for this effect, as the sloppier the shuffle looks, the better. You should practice it, though, in order to do it rapidly, thus convincing the audience that you have really mixed face-up cards with face-down cards all through the pack. Your rapid action will be hard to follow, (so if a spectator tries to duplicate your shuffle, the cards really will be mixed up).

SELF-REVERSING PACK – OUTDONE

EFFECT

A card is selected, noted, and returned to the pack, which is then shuffled by the magician in an apparently ordinary manner. Holding the deck in both hands, the magician gives the pack a very peculiar "slip-slop" shuffle, carelessly mixing face-up cards with face-down cards creating a hopeless jumble. After a single magic tap, the pack is spread on the table, showing that all the cards in the deck have turned face down, with one exception: the chosen card is face up in the center of the pack.

METHOD

1 Have the spectator return the selected card to the deck and, using one of the methods you have learned (see pages 25, 33, and 63), control the card to the bottom of the pack. This can be done effectively by bringing the card to the top of the pack using the HINDU SHUFFLE PICK-UP CONTROL (see page 26). From there, the card can be brought to the bottom by the OVER-HAND SHUFFLE – TOP CARD TO BOTTOM (see page 33).

Another neat way to accomplish this is to have the card returned to the pack in the course of the HINDU SHUFFLE (see page 19). As the card is replaced, you glimpse the bottom card (HINDU GLIMPSE, see page 20), which then becomes your key card. Give the pack a few single cuts, apparently losing the card completely. Next, look through the pack and say you will try to find the chosen card, which you actually will do, thanks to the key card. Run through the deck, holding the cards so that only you can see their faces. When you come to the chosen card, shake your head and say that you just can't find it. Tell the audience that you will do another trick instead. Ask the spectator to remember the card anyway, because you may be able to locate it later on. With that, you cut the pack, bringing the chosen card to the top of the face-up pack. Turn the pack over so the chosen card is the bottom card of the face-down pack.

NOTE: Whichever method you use, be careful when you turn the pack face down, so that no one sees that the chosen card is on the bottom.

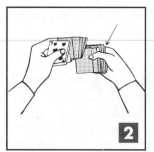

2 With the chosen card at the bottom of the deck, begin the "slip-slop" shuffle (already described in the SELF-REVERSING PACK, see page 74), repeatedly sliding off batches of cards (some face up, some face down) from the left hand into the right hand.

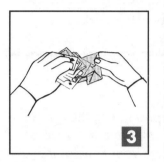

3 The slip-slop shuffle is continued until only a few cards remain in your right hand. Then, when the left hand is in its thumb downward position, the right thumb pushes the cards remaining in the right hand onto the bottom of the pack, except for the bottom "selected" card (indicated in the illustrations by an "X") which is still held in the right hand.

4 After the left hand turns over (thumb upward), the right hand places its single card (the chosen card, X) on top of the pack, beneath the left thumb, as though to complete the hit-or-miss shuffle, which now looks sloppy indeed.

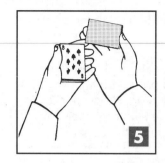

5 Square the deck, remarking that the cards are hopelessly mixed, as you proceed to cut the pack (once near the top and once near the bottom) to show how some cards are face to back and some back to face, as described in the SELF-REVERSING PACK (see page 74).

6 With the last cut, repeat the procedure where you divide the pack between the back-to-back sections and reassemble the deck. All the cards in the pack will now be face down, except for the chosen card (X), which is face up in the center of the pack.

7 Immediately spread the pack face down on the table, showing all backs except for the single face-up chosen card in the middle!

GRANT'S SUPERIOR CARD TRICK

Practically every magician over the past thirty or more years has performed at least a few (and often many) of U.F. "Gen" Grant's magical creations. Many of the current books on magic owe at least a portion of their content to concepts originated by the brilliant talent of this conceiver of conjuring cleverness. Here is a triple mystery created by "Gen" Grant, whose ingenious card effects are becoming classics.

In this particular effect, the magician starts by pretending to show the spectators how a trick is done, an excellent way of misleading them so that they miss the real secret. From there, the trick builds to the triple climax. This trick should usually be reserved for a spectator who has some small knowledge of magic, and perhaps is aware of the key card principle. In this case, a little knowledge turns out to be a very baffling thing.

EFFECT

The magician has a spectator select a card and replace it in the pack. The magician then shows the audience how easily a selected card can be found by simply noting the card above it and watching for that card to appear when the pack is dealt. Proceeding along that line, the magician deals the chosen card face down to the spectator, and then deals any other card to another person. The magician keeps the key card. But when the faces of the three cards are shown, all have magically changed places.

SECRET AND PREPARATION

A The only special item needed is an extra card with the same back design as the pack that you intend to use. This extra card is a duplicate of a card already in the pack. Assuming that the duplicate card is a four of diamonds, remove the regular four of diamonds from the pack and place both cards on the bottom of the deck. (In the illustrations, we will call the bottom four "A" and the next four, "B.")

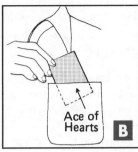

B Also remove one other card (any one you want) from the deck. (For the illustrations, we will use the ace of hearts.) Place this card in your shirt pocket with its back toward the audience. You do not even have to know the name of this card.

METHOD

1 To begin, spread the pack face down and ask a spectator to take a card, explaining that you will "teach" the spectator how to do a trick. (In the illustrations, the selected card is marked with an "X," and we will assume that it is the six of spades.)

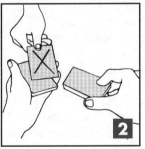

2 While the spectator is looking at the card, square the pack and begin a regular Hindu shuffle by drawing off half the pack in your left hand. Tell the spectator to replace the card (X) on that half of the pack.

3 Next, deliberately turn the right-hand packet face up, showing the four of diamonds (A) on the bottom of the packet. Say, "All you have to do in order to find any selected card is to secretly note the bottom card of the upper packet before you place it on top of the selected card. The four of diamonds will be my secret locator in this trick."

4 Place the right-hand packet face down on the left-hand packet. Call the audience's attention to the fact that this places the locator card (A) next to the spectator's card (X). Remind the viewers that your locator card is the four of diamonds and tell them to watch for it as you deal the cards.

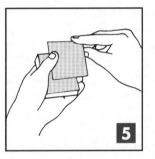

5 Holding the pack in your left hand, begin dealing cards, one at a time.

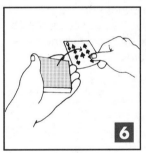

6 Deal the cards face up on the table, placing each card on the one before. You can do this rapidly at first.

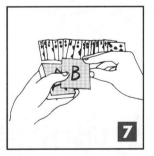

7 Slow down as you near the center of the pack. Continue dealing until you reach the first four of diamonds (B). The other duplicate four (A) is just below it, the top card of the packet you hold in your left hand.

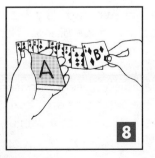

8 When you turn over the first four of diamonds (B), deal it on the row of face up cards, saying, "That's my locator card, the four of diamonds, which means your card is next."

9 Unknown to the spectator, the next card is the duplicate four of diamonds (A), which the spectator naturally assumes to be the chosen card (X), since the spectator saw you place the four of diamonds just above it.

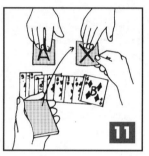

10 Deal the top card (A) on the table in front of the spectator, saying, "There is your card, just below the four of diamonds, so I want you to keep your hand on it." The spectator does, never suspecting that instead of the chosen card (S), it is really the duplicate four of diamonds (A).

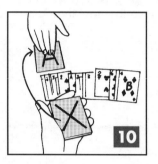

11 Next, turn to another person and deal the next card (X) face down on the table in front of this other person. Ask this person to put a hand on it. State that since no one knows what this card is, you will call it the mystery card. Actually, it is the card chosen by the first spectator, the six of spades (X).

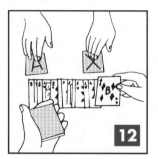

12 Say to the first spectator, "You now have your card, which you alone know." Turn to the second person and add, "And you have the mystery card, which nobody knows." Pick up the face-up four of diamonds (B) from the row, saying, "Since everybody knows my card, I'll put it in my pocket."

13 With that, turn the back of your four toward the spectators and slide it into your shirt pocket with your right hand.

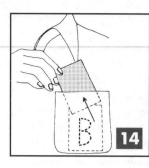

14 In the same move, grip the card that you placed in the pocket beforehand and bring it out immediately. Glance at it with a puzzled frown.

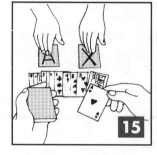

15 Say, "Wait! This isn't my card!" Turn to the first spectator and add, "It must be your card!" With that, turn the card face up, showing it to be an ordinary card (as in the illustrations), the ace of hearts.

16 Have the first spectator turn over the card on the table. The spectator will be amazed to find that instead of the chosen card, the six of spades (X), it is your locator card, the four of diamonds (A). Say, "Why, that's my card! What was your card?"

17 The spectator will answer, "The six of spades." With that, turn to the second person and say, "Let's see your mystery card, the one that nobody knows." The second spectator turns it over, revealing the first spectator's chosen card, the six of spades (X). This is the card whose name the first spectator has just revealed for the first time, which so far as the spectator knew, was a secret! The climax is complete!

COMMENTS AND SUGGESTIONS

This is not really a three-way change, because only two cards, the one chosen by the first spectator and the card you showed as your locator, actually change places. The fact that the second person's "mystery card" is missing and you come up with the odd card is sufficient to make it look like a magical round robin.

Revealing the ordinary card immediately is very important: before suspicion can be aroused, you spring the twin surprises of the locator card and the selected card, both showing up where they don't belong. The cleverest part is that your duplicate locator (B), the four of diamonds, is safely hidden in your shirt pocket, leaving only a complete pack to be examined by the spectators.

CHAPTER 11

FLOURISHES

Fancy flourishes with cards date far back to the self-styled "Kard Kings" of the vaudeville era. Houdini himself had lithographs showing him performing a myriad of masterful card flourishes.

One thing is certain, card flourishes are sure to impress your audience. Whatever practice you give to such manipulations is time well spent. Your audience will recognize your skill and respect it.

The more you practice them, the more your card work will improve in general, making your entire performance more effective.

ONE-HAND CUT – BASIC METHOD

To many people, the sign of a real card expert is the ability to "cut" a pack of cards using only one hand. It appears to be a difficult maneuver, but it's really much easier than it looks.

METHOD

All of the illustrations are from the audience's point of view. The deck is held in the left hand.

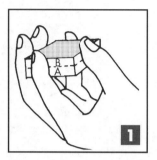

1 Hold the pack between the tips of your thumb and fingers, as shown. Your first finger and little finger are at the opposite ends of the pack. Your other fingers and thumb are at the sides, as shown. Be sure your thumb and fingers point almost straight up. Hold the deck at the tips of your fingers to form a deep "well" between the deck and the palm of your hand.

2 To begin, bend your thumb just enough to let the lower half of the deck drop into the palm of your cupped hand. (We will refer to this lower half as Packet A.) The upper half (Packet B) remains held between the tips of your thumb and your two middle fingers. Your little finger will help to keep the cards from sliding out of your hand.

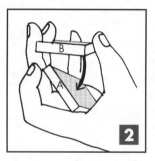

3 Bring your first finger below the lower half (Packet A) and push the packet upward, sliding it along the bottom card of the upper half (Packet B).

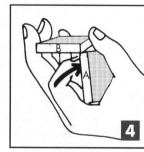

4 Continue pushing the edge of the lower half (Packet A) all the way up to your thumb, as shown.

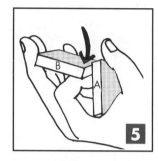

5 Gently extend your fingers just enough to allow the edges of the two halves to clear, so that your thumb releases Packet B, which drops on top of your curled first finger.

6 By curling your first finger lower into your hand, Packet B will come down with it. Packet B now becomes the lower half.

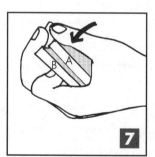

7 Slowly begin closing up your hand, bringing both halves together, with Packet A on top of Packet B.

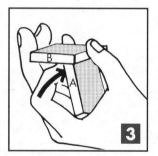

8 Extend your first finger around the end of the pack, squaring the halves into place. You have just done a ONE-HAND CUT!

COMMENTS AND SUGGESTIONS

Although this flourish appears to be quite difficult, once you take the deck in your hand and follow the steps as shown in the pictures, you will find the ONE-HAND CUT quite easy to do. It is best, particularly when first learning, to use the narrow, bridge-size cards rather than the wider poker-size cards. After you have mastered the sleight, you may wish to try it with the larger cards. You can also begin to practice the variations that follow.

ONE-HAND CUT — FIRST VARIATION

This is the first of two variations of the ONE-HAND CUT — BASIC METHOD, enabling you to display your dexterity while also serving as a step toward other card manipulations involving the same basic sleight.

EFFECT

Holding a pack of cards in one hand, the magician starts a simple ONE-HAND CUT (see page 80), but pauses during the early stage to turn it into a three-way cut. The magician transposes the bottom, center, and top portions of the pack. This makes an impressive ornamental flourish when the three sections drop neatly into place.

METHOD

NOTE: In all ONE-HAND CUTS, you may hold the deck in either your right or your left hand, whichever is easier for you. All of the illustrations are from the spectator's view with the deck held in the left hand.

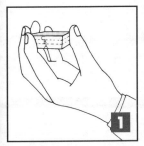

1 Begin by holding the pack in the same position as you did for the regular ONE-HAND CUT. Your first finger and little finger are at opposite ends of the pack; your two middle fingers and thumb are at the sides. Be sure that your fingers and thumb point up, or slightly to the right, if this is easier for you. Be certain, as before, that you have formed a deep well between the deck and the palm of your hand.

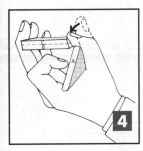

2 Unlike the regular ONE-HAND CUT, where the pack is cut into two equal sections, in this modified version, begin by bending your thumb just enough to let the lower third (Packet A) of the deck drop into your cupped hand. Your little finger will help to keep the cards from sliding out of your hand.

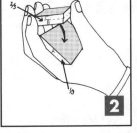

3 Bring your first finger below Packet A and begin pushing its edge upward toward your thumb, as shown.

4 Continue pushing Packet A all the way up to your left thumb. The top edge of Packet A will contact your thumb near the bend of the first joint of the thumb.

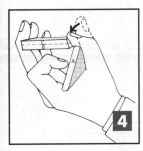

5 Your hand now holds the bulk of the deck between the tip of the thumb and your fingers, while the bottom third of the deck (Packet

A) is held between the bend of your thumb and the palm of your hand, as shown in Step 4.

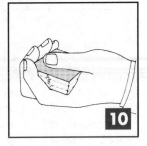

6 With the cards held firmly in this position, relax the tip of your left thumb, allowing the middle third of the deck (Packet B) to drop from the bulk of the pack into your cupped hand.

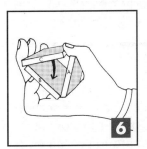

7 Once again, bring your first finger below Packet B and push it upward toward your thumb until it is all the way up against the bottom of Packet A. The remaining third of the deck, Packet C, is still being held by the tips of your thumb and fingers, as shown.

8 Release your thumb tip from Packet C and allow its top to clear the top edge of Packets A and

B. You can help the packets to clear by pushing the bottom of Packet B with your first finger. Packet C will come down with it into your palm. Packet C now becomes the lower third of the packet.

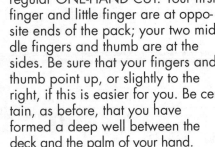

9 Slowly begin closing up your hand, bringing all three sections together to complete the cut.

10 Finally, extend your first finger around the end of the pack and square the deck as the sections settle into place. You have just executed the ONE-HAND CUT — FIRST VARIATION.

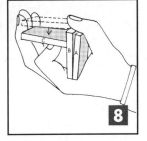

COMMENTS AND SUGGESTIONS

Practice this flourish with a narrow, bridge-size pack. It is much easier to handle than the wider poker-size deck. Later, you can switch to the wider size, if your fingers are long enough to handle it easily. The dropping of the center section, Packet B, is the vital point, because your thumb must hold both Packets A and C in place until your first finger releases Packet B. If Packet A should accidentally drop during that maneuver, that's OK, just let it fall on top of Packet B and complete what would then be a slightly different cut than you had originally planned.

ONE-HAND CUT – SECOND VARIATION

This is another variation of the ONE-HAND CUT (see page 80) that can be used interchangeably with the one already described. The two cuts can also be worked in combination, starting with one, and ending with the other, all in the same sequence.

EFFECT

In this triple cut, the magician divides the lower section into two packets and lets the upper third drop in between. This can be repeated several times, either in slow motion, or at a rapid speed once the knack is acquired. Either way, it increases the audience's admiration of the magician's skill.

METHOD

1 In the usual ONE-HAND CUT style, hold the pack between the tips of the thumb and fingers of either hand. The first finger and little finger are at opposite ends of the pack, the other fingers and thumb are at the sides. Be sure the fingers point straight up (or nearly straight up, if this is easier for you). Just be sure to form a deep well between the deck and the palm of your hand.

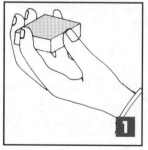

2 To begin, bend the thumb just enough to let the lower 2/3 of the pack drop into the cupped hand. The little finger will help to keep the cards from sliding out of your hand.

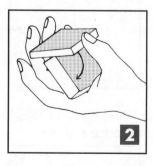

3 Bring your first finger below the bulk of the pack and push its edge upward, sliding it along the bottom of the upper third of the pack. Continue pushing the lower section all the way up to the ball of the thumb, as shown.

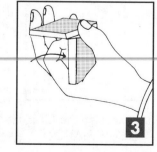

4 Your left thumb retains hold of half of the bulk of the pack, as you begin to open your first finger, allowing the other half to drop back into your hand.

5 As the packet falls into your hand, relax the grip of the tip of your thumb on the top third of the pack and allow this packet to fall into the hand between the two packets already formed.

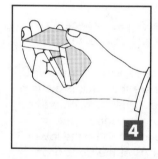

6 Slowly begin closing up your hand, bringing all three packets together to complete the cut. Finally, extend your first finger around the end of the pack and square the pack as the three packets settle into place. You have just executed the ONE-HAND CUT – SECOND VARIATION.

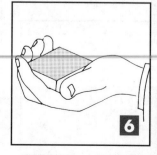

COMMENTS AND SUGGESTIONS

Along with serving as an ornamental flourish, this variation of the ONE-HAND CUT fulfills a useful purpose. With it, you can "bury" the top card of the pack somewhere in the middle of the deck. As you call attention to that fact, the audience doesn't realize that the bottom card remains the same and can, therefore, be used as a key card in a trick that follows.

RIBBON SPREAD

EFFECT

In performing card tricks, it is often necessary to spread the entire pack of cards across the table so that all of their backs or faces are visible to the spectators. The following describes the method for executing a RIBBON SPREAD which looks very nice and demonstrates your ability to handle cards skillfully.

METHOD

NOTE: *The RIBBON SPREAD is difficult to do on a slick or hard surface. However, it is quite easy on a soft, textured surface such as a felt-top table, a rug, a heavy table cloth or a magician's "close-up mat."*

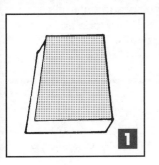

1 Place the deck on the table, face down, slightly bevelled at the side of the deck, as shown.

2 Lay all four fingers of your right hand across the top of the pack, with the tips of the fingers extending over the bevelled edge.

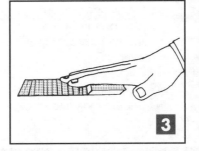

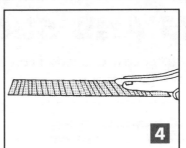

3 With a slight downward pressure of the hand, move your arm and hand to the right. The cards will begin to spread apart evenly from the bottom of the pack as you slide the bulk of the pack along the table.

4 Continue this sliding motion, releasing cards from the bottom of the pack until all of the cards are evenly spread in a ribbon pattern along the table.

COMMENTS AND SUGGESTIONS

In practicing the RIBBON SPREAD, be sure you have a soft surface and remember that the sliding motion of the hand must be smooth and unbroken in order to achieve even spacing between the individual cards. The motion should not be done too slowly. A moderately fast movement produces the best results. As always, practice is the key to success.

RIBBON SPREAD TURNOVER

This is an ideal flourish to use when doing card tricks at a table. Though easily learned, it gives the impression that you are displaying great skill. Always take advantage of such opportunities, because they create a lasting impression on the audience regarding your work. It's all part of the game called magic.

EFFECT

The magician takes an ordinary pack of cards and spreads them in an even row face down along the table. Then, by tilting up one end of the spread, the magician causes the entire row of cards to turn face up!

METHOD

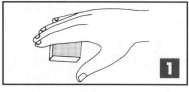

1 Set the pack face down on the table in preparation for the RIBBON SPREAD (see page 83).

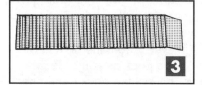

2 RIBBON SPREAD the pack from left to right, as described earlier. The cards in the spread must be evenly spaced. Any gaps or breaks in the spread will disrupt the turnover.

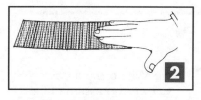

3 The completed spread should look like this.

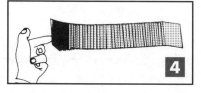

4 With your left fingers, raise the outer edge of the card on the left end of the spread, tilting it up on its edge, as shown.

5 Rotate the card on its edge until it turns over (face up), causing all of the cards above it to turn over in sequence.

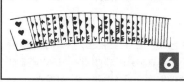

6 The turnover will progress throughout the spread until all of the cards are face up, as shown.

COMMENTS AND SUGGESTIONS

This is the basic turnover, a rather easy and most impressive flourish. To add even more to your display of skill, you can incorporate the two following variations.

REVERSE METHOD

After completing the above, you may immediately reverse the procedure.

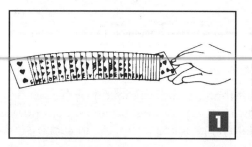

1 With your right hand, lift the card at the far right end of the now face-up spread. Using this card as the "pusher" card, pivot it on its edge.

2 This causes the cards to repeat the turnover.

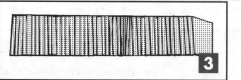

3 This time, they return to their original face-down position.

COMMENTS AND SUGGESTIONS

By placing your left hand at the left end of the spread and your right hand at the right end of the spread, you can "flip-flop" the cards back and forth as they turn over in rotation—first, face up, then face down—making not only a remarkable display of skill, but also a very pretty picture.

TURNOVER CONTROL

This is another even more intriguing use of the turnover. It is particularly effective when used between effects in your card routine. This is also a most spectacular way of showing that the deck is ordinary and composed of "all different" cards.

METHOD

1 First, remove any card from the deck and place it on the table. Perform Steps 1 through 5 in the RIBBON SPREAD TURNOVER (see page 84). When the cards have turned to approximately the middle of the spread, pick up the card you removed and hold it, as shown, in your right hand. This card will be used to control the sequence of the turnover.

2 You will find that, as you carefully touch the edge of the single card in your right hand to the "peak" of the turnover, you can very easily control the sequence and direction of the turnover. For

instance, you can now reverse the turnover by moving the single card back to the left, as shown. As you move the card to the left, keep the edge of the card touching the new, constantly changing peak. This can be done back and forth as often as you wish, as long as the cards remain evenly spread on the table.

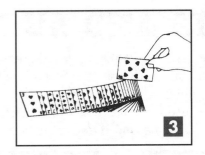

3 The single card is then used to control the turnover all the way over to the right end of the spread, where the cards will fall face up as they did at the conclusion of the regular RIBBON SPREAD TURNOVER.

PRESSURE FAN

Giving your performance a professional look should be a primary aim when taking up card magic. Shuffles and cuts should all be done smoothly and neatly, as a prelude to fancier moves. This applies specifically to the PRESSURE FAN.

EFFECT

Holding the squared pack in one hand, the magician deftly spreads it in a circular fashion across the fingers of the other hand, finally displaying it in a broad fan with the index corners of the cards showing evenly throughout its colorful span.

METHOD

1 Hold the pack by the ends between the tips of the right thumb and fingers. Your thumb is at the center of the lower end and your first, second, and third fingers are across the upper end. Your little finger rests lightly on the side of the deck.

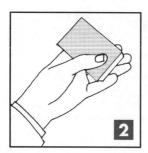

2 With the cards held firmly in the right hand, place the pack against the fingers of the left hand in the position shown. The ball of the left thumb rests at the middle of the lower end of the pack. (The right hand is not shown in the illustration in order to show more clearly the exact position in which the pack is held against the left hand by the right hand.)

3 To begin the fan, squeeze the fingers of your right hand downward, bending the cards over the left forefinger.

4 This is the audience's view as you begin the fan.

5 In one continuous motion, allow the cards to start "springing" from the right fingertips, as the right hand begins to rotate the pack to the right. The left thumb acts as a pivot point, holding the lower left corner of the pack.

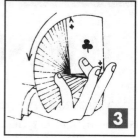

6 Continue the circular motion of the right hand around the tips of the left fingers and down the side of the left hand.

7 Continue to "spring release" cards in succession until the fan is complete. (This action is shown from the audience's point of view.)

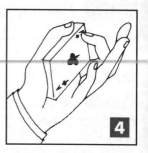

COMMENTS AND SUGGESTIONS

The amount of pressure necessary to make the fan depends on the pack you are using. A brand new, high-quality pack can be fanned with a light touch, but it will need more bending pressure from the right thumb and fingers. With a new, "clean" deck, the cards are smooth enough to spread evenly and stiff enough to resist pressure. The more a pack is shuffled and used, the more flexible it becomes. The pressure must be decreased proportionately. As the deck becomes soiled, it becomes more and more difficult to get the cards evenly spaced.

CLOSING THE FAN – ONE-HAND METHOD

The simple action of closing the PRESSURE FAN can be as impressive as the fan itself, particularly when it is executed without the aid of the other hand!

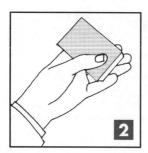

1 Begin by forming a PRESSURE FAN, as described previously. Four fingers should be flat against the face of the pack with the thumb pressing inward at the pivot point on the back of the fan.

2 To close the fan, shift your left first finger so that its fingertip rests on the face of the first card as

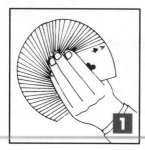

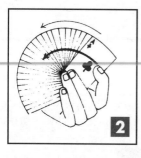

close to the outer edge of the fan as possible.

3 With a slight amount of pressure from your left first finger on the face card of the deck, begin to push your finger in a circular motion, upward and to the right, as you slowly begin to close the fan.

4 Continue pushing the fan closed. Open the remaining fingers of the left hand when necessary, allowing the first finger to sweep the cards downward as they collect in succession against the heel of the hand, until the fan is closed.

ONE-HAND FAN

♥ Though basically a card flourish, this is also a useful move in connection with various tricks. That makes two good reasons why you should practice it.

EFFECT

Holding a pack of cards face front between the thumb and fingers of the right hand, the magician, with one deft move, instantly spreads the pack in a broad fan, showing the index corners of the cards in a colorful fashion. Closing the fan and turning the pack over, the magician fans them again, showing the backs spread evenly, allowing a spectator to select a card. This is an excellent opening move for many card effects.

METHOD

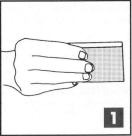

1 Hold the pack in your right hand with your thumb on the face of the pack and your fingers flat against the back. Position your thumb at the lower right-hand corner of the pack, as shown.

2 Here is a view of the pack from the other side. Notice that your fingers only cover half the length of the pack.

3 In one smooth, continuous motion, start to slide your thumb upward. At the same time, curl your fingers inward and downward, as the pack begins to spread out in the form of a fan.

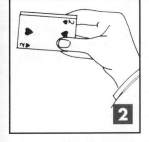

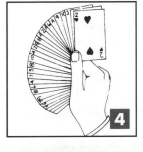

4 Continue sliding your thumb upward as the fingers continue pushing the cards in a sort of "smearing" motion down the heel of the hand, until they curl into the palm, almost forming a fist with the cards held tightly between. When your thumb and fingers have reached this position, the fan should be fully formed, as shown.

5 Your fingers are responsible for forming the lower half of the fan, and the thumb is responsible for forming the upper half.

6 Here is a view of the completed fan from the other side. Notice the right fingers have curled into the palm of the hand to form a fist.

COMMENTS AND SUGGESTIONS

In tricks where you are using half a pack or less, fanning is just as effective as with a full pack. All the cards in the half packet can be spread out evenly and more of each card will show. Even when doing a trick with only a few cards, such as the FOUR ACES, using a ONE-HAND FAN to show their faces has a striking effect and adds to your style as a performer. You may also wish to learn the fan with both hands. Then, by splitting the deck and holding half in each hand, the two fans will form a truly spectacular display.

Do not be disappointed if you cannot master the ONE-HAND FAN immediately. Careful practice will teach you exactly how much pressure to exert with the thumb and fingers in order for the cards to distribute properly from the top and bottom of the pack, forming an evenly spaced fan.

GLOSSARY

The following is a list of definitions of words and terms used in this book. Each is listed with either a brief definition or a reference to the page where the particular sleight or term is described.

BACK: The back of a card is the pattern or picture on the opposite side of the face. The back design is repeated on all the cards of the deck.

BOTTOM OF THE DECK: The *lowermost* card or portion of the deck.

BRIDGE-SIZE DECK: A deck of cards slightly smaller than a poker deck, measuring 2-1/4" wide. Bridge-size cards are frequently used and give the magician an advantage in certain tricks because of their smaller width.

CARD DISCOVERY: The climax or end of many card tricks during which the spectator's card is revealed or produced in a "magical" manner.

CARD LOCATION: Any method that allows the magician to find or locate a selected card after it has been returned to the pack.

CONTROL: Any method (usually unknown to the audience) that allows the performer to move a particular card or cards to a specific location in the pack. This term is used extensively in this book. In almost every instance, it refers to the return to the pack of the selected card by the spectator and the magician's ability to "control" the placement of the card and its location within the deck (top, bottom, etc.).

CUTTING THE DECK:

    SINGLE CUT: Removing a packet of cards from the top of the deck, placing it beside the lower portion, and then completing the cut by placing the lower portion on top of the upper portion.

    DOUBLE OR MULTIPLE CUT: Dividing the deck into more than two stacks and then reassembling the deck.

    FALSE CUT: Any cut that leaves the deck in the same order as it was before the cut.

DEAL THE CARDS: Removing cards from the pack, singly or in groups. This can be done with one or two hands.

DEUCE: Another name for a two.

DOVETAIL SHUFFLE: See page 10.

FACE CARDS, PICTURE CARDS, OR COURT CARDS: All of the jacks, queens, and kings.

FACE: The face of a card shows its value and suit.

FALSE SHUFFLE: Any shuffle that leaves the deck in the same order as it was before the shuffle.

FAN OF CARDS: A number of cards held in the shape of a fan.

FLASH: Allowing the spectator to briefly see the face of any card.

FLOURISH: A display of skill with the cards. Flourishes are usually not tricks, although they can become important parts of some effects. Examples of flourishes are Fanning the Pack, the Ribbon Spread, One-Hand Cuts, etc.

FORCE: Causing a spectator to select a particular card or cards when the spectator thinks the choice was freely made.

FULL DECK: Fifty-two cards, consisting of four suits (diamonds, clubs, hearts, and spades), with 13 cards per suit from ace through king. The joker is an optional 53rd card.

GIANT CARD: An extra large card that is usually four times larger than a regular poker-size playing card.

GIMMICK: Any secret device used to perform a trick. The audience is usually not aware of a gimmick.

GLIMPSE: Secretly noting a card while holding or shuffling the pack. See page 20.

KEY CARD: Any card that can be used as a locator card.

LOCATOR CARD: Any card that can be used as a key to find some other card in the pack. An example of a locator card is a short card (see page 62).

MAGIC LOOP, THE: Double-stick cellophane tape, which has a sticky surface on both sides, is useful in many magic effects, particularly if the audience is unaware of its presence. If you wish to do tricks that call for double-stick tape and do not have any on hand, you can easily make your own by forming a "Magic Loop." This is done by taking a piece of regular, single-side tape and forming it into a loop with the sticky side out. Place this on whatever surface you want to apply the tape to, and by pressing the loop flat, you will have formed the equivalent of a piece of double-stick tape.

MECHANIC'S GRIP: A method used for holding the deck in the left hand for dealing. The left first finger extends around the front of the deck.

MOVE: A "move" may be either secret, in which case it is a sleight, or some movement of the cards that the spectators can see such as cutting the deck.

ONE-WAY DECK: This is usually a picture-back deck in which the back patterns may all be arranged so that they face one way. This type of deck may be quickly made into a trick deck by arranging the picture backs so that they are all facing one way. After a card has been selected, the deck is merely turned around so that when the card is returned, its picture is facing in the opposite direction. Then, by looking quickly through the pack at the backs, the selected card can easily be found.

PATTERN-BACK DECK: Any deck with a pattern or geometrical design on its back.

PICTURE-BACK DECK: Any deck with a picture on its back. The picture may be of anything, such as a dog, a cat, or the Grand Canyon. Since these are mostly novelty cards, they are usually not well suited for magic effects, except in special instances such as card fans.

POKER-SIZE DECK: A deck of standard-size playing cards, measuring 2-1/2" wide.

PREARRANGED DECK: A deck that has been set up or arranged in some special order before the performance.

REVERSED CARD: Any card that is face up in a face-down pack (or face down in a face-up pack).

SET-UP: Any preparation done before a show (or in many cases during a performance) that arranges the cards in a special order or location.

SLEIGHT: A secret move done with the cards that is not known to the spectators, such as Double Lift, Glide, etc.

SPOT CARDS: Any card from ace through ten in any suit.

STANDARD DEALING POSITION: The pack is held in the left hand, resting on the palm. The fingers extend around the right edge of the pack; the thumb is on top. From this position, the thumb is ready to push off cards across the tips of the fingers, so that the right hand can draw or deal each card away.

STANDARD DEAL: Cards are drawn off, one at a time, face downward, and placed on the table. Each card goes on the card that was dealt before it. This reverses the order of the cards.

STOCK: Any portion of the pack containing cards that have been set up in a special order.

TOP OF DECK: When the deck is face down, the *uppermost* card or portion of the deck.

TREY: Another name for a three.

TURN-UP DEAL: The cards are dealt singly from the top of the face-down deck, but they are turned face up as they are dealt. This does not reverse the order of the deck.

WHITE BORDER-BACK DECK: Most pattern-backed cards have a white border around the outer edge. (One notable exception is the "Bee" brand deck.) A white border-back deck is essential in the performance of many of the tricks described in this book because, when a card from this type of deck is reversed (turned face up in a face-down deck), it will not be noticeable because the white edges of the face are the same as the white border on the pattern-back.